Making Metal Jewelry

Erin —
Forge ahead
with passion and
love !
Nancy Lee

by Nancy Lee

ALPHA

A member of Penguin Group (USA) Inc.

This book is dedicated to those in pursuit of bringing dreams to life in metal. In your journey, you expand the craft. May it ever be so.

ALPHA BOOKS

Published by Penguin Group (USA) Inc.

Penguin Group (USA) Inc., 375 Hudson Street, New York, New York 10014, USA • Penguin Group (Canada), 90 Eglinton Avenue East, Suite 700, Toronto, Ontario M4P 2Y3, Canada (a division of Pearson Penguin Canada Inc.) • Penguin Books Ltd., 80 Strand, London WC2R 0RL, England • Penguin Ireland, 25 St. Stephen's Green, Dublin 2, Ireland (a division of Penguin Books Ltd.) • Penguin Group (Australia), 250 Camberwell Road, Camberwell, Victoria 3124, Australia (a division of Pearson Australia Group Pty. Ltd.) • Penguin Books India Pvt. Ltd., 11 Community Centre, Panchsheel Park, New Delhi—110 017, India • Penguin Group (NZ), 67 Apollo Drive, Rosedale, North Shore, Auckland 1311, New Zealand (a division of Pearson New Zealand Ltd.) • Penguin Books (South Africa) (Pty.) Ltd., 24 Sturdee Avenue, Rosebank, Johannesburg 2196, South Africa • Penguin Books Ltd., Registered Offices: 80 Strand, London WC2R 0RL, England

International Standard Book Number: 978-1-61564-272-4
Library of Congress Catalog Card Number: 2013933128

15 14 13   8 7 6 5 4 3 2 1

Interpretation of the printing code: The rightmost number of the first series of numbers is the year of the book's printing; the rightmost number of the second series of numbers is the number of the book's printing. For example, a printing code of 13-1 shows that the first printing occurred in 2013.

Note: This publication contains the opinions and ideas of its author. It is intended to provide helpful and informative material on the subject matter covered. It is sold with the understanding that the author and publisher are not engaged in rendering professional services in the book. If the reader requires personal assistance or advice, a competent professional should be consulted. The author and publisher specifically disclaim any responsibility for any liability, loss, or risk, personal or otherwise, which is incurred as a consequence, directly or indirectly, of the use and application of any of the contents of this book.

Most Alpha books are available at special quantity discounts for bulk purchases for sales promotions, premiums, fund-raising, or educational use. Special books, or book excerpts, can also be created to fit specific needs. For details, write: Special Markets, Alpha Books, 375 Hudson Street, New York, NY 10014.

Publisher: Mike Sanders

Executive Managing Editor: Billy Fields

Executive Acquisitions Editor: Lori Cates Hand

Senior Production Editor: Janette Lynn

Senior Designer: Rebecca Batchelor

Layout: Brian Massey

Indexer: Celia McCoy

Proofreader: Jan Zoya

ALWAYS LEARNING   PEARSON

Contents

Appendixes

Introduction

I fell into metal by accident. I had signed up for a jewelry-making class. My only goal was to learn how to fabricate earwires and clasps. I wanted something of a high quality to complement my handmade polymer clay beads. My instructor recommended sterling silver, so I bought some. That's when it started ….

Learning to love metal was easy. Learning to work with it was, and continues to be, an exciting game. It required me to learn a variety of techniques and apply them in numerous ways. It required "elastic thinking." And it still does. Every day, I stretch.

With this book, you can take what you already know and expand on it. Using your hands and tools, you'll try things out. You might not have access to all of the tools, chemicals, materials, or supplies to execute the techniques in the exact way I suggest. So you'll use "elastic thinking" to come up with a genius workaround: adapt a tool, find supplies in your kitchen or garage, or alter a portion of your design in order to proceed with your creation. The stretch is part and parcel of fine craft. And I mean "craft" in its highest and best form!

Join the ancient league of the metalsmith. Become a member in the elastic thinkers club. Get a full pass to the inner circle. The goal of this book is to enable to you bring your dreams to life in metal. Make it how you can. Make it first in your dreams, your heart, and your mind, and then with your hands.

How This Book Is Organized

This book is organized into three main parts. Even if you've made some metal jewelry before, I encourage you to review the first two parts before beginning the projects in the third part of the book. In metalsmithing, one thing builds upon another. To keep from repeating a lot of the same techniques in several places throughout the book, you'll often be referred to the section in which that technique first appears. Getting familiar with the sections will help you have more fun with the projects that come later.

Chapters 1 through 4 establish some ground-level basics: establishing a workspace, gathering tools and materials, understanding the properties of metal, and creating jewelry designs.

Chapters 5 through 13 start you on the road to making jewelry from shaping and cutting metal to adding texture, color, and embellishments and polishing your final piece to perfection.

Chapter 14 does just that. What you already know and what you've learned about working with metal come together in these 10 enjoyable projects. You'll get lots of options for making them your own way, too.

Extras

I know a lot of things that fall into the tidbit category. To make good use of this important information, you'll receive many tasty morsels under the following headings:

> **DEFINITION**
>
> Words that might be unfamiliar to you but are commonly used in metalsmithing and jewelry making are defined here.

> **SAFE 'SMITHING**
>
> These notes call out known safety issues and ways to maintain a safe studio, healthy body, and green environment.

> **ARTISAN TIP**
>
> These notes provide tips, tricks, and materials to try, along with design suggestions. Metalsmithing offers lots of ways to do the same thing. You'll see alternate techniques and other uses for tools here, too.

> **METAL MISHAP**
>
> Tear-free ways to prevent and fix common mistakes.

But Wait! There's More!

Have you logged on to idiotsguides.com lately? If you haven't, go there now! As a bonus to the book, we've included two additional jewelry projects and reference information that you'll want to check out, all online. Point your browser to idiotsguides.com/metaljewelry, and enjoy!

Acknowledgments

I stand on the shoulders of the metalsmiths who have gone before me. Those who have taught, shared, advised, written books and white papers, and posted tips on Facebook (especially the Metalsmiths Unite 2.0 group), thank you. These teachings are a part of me, and without them, I'd have nothing to dream with. With them, this offering is possible.

This book could not have been written without the loving support of my sisters, Janet Thorlton and Teresa Morrison. They are my hot-pink beacons of light and endless inspiration. Thanks to my parents, Lee and Roseanne Sherman, for enrolling me in art classes at eight years old, and for allowing me to march to the beat of my own drum. To my son, Brad Lee, who is an artist at heart and who inspires me to be a better person. Thank you to Wug Laku, for his steadfast support and for a thousand studio photos. Thanks to Paul D'Andrea for his inspired photography and to Lisa Swieczkowski for her help in the studio. Extra special thanks to Krista Bermeo of Krista Bermeo Studio and Larry and Jeryl Mitch for their friendship and hospitality during sequestered writing sessions, and thanks also goes to LaVreen Hall of Just Words, for her incredible wisdom and insight.

Thanks also go out to my wonderful editing staff for helping bring my voice to life: Lori Cates Hand, acquisitions editor extraordinaire, Christy Wagner, editorial supervisor, and Rebecca Batchelor, senior designer, and the many other talented folks at Alpha Books. Your support and enthusiasm for this book astounded me!

Special Thanks to the Technical Reviewer

The Complete Idiot's Guide to Making Metal Jewelry was reviewed by an expert who double-checked the accuracy of what you'll learn here, to help us ensure this book gives you everything you need to know about crafting your own metal masterpieces. Special thanks are extended to Ginger Meek Allen.

Ginger is a studio jeweler and metalsmith with two decades of experience in jewelry making of all kinds. Her work is collected widely. She regularly uses all the techniques explored in this book.

Trademarks

All terms mentioned in this book that are known to be or are suspected of being trademarks or service marks have been appropriately capitalized. Alpha Books and Penguin Group (USA) Inc. cannot attest to the accuracy of this information. Use of a term in this book should not be regarded as affecting the validity of any trademark or service mark.

Setting Up Your Workspace

In This Chapter

- The metal attraction
- Workspace requirements
- Organization tips
- Work surface options
- Safety in the studio

This chapter introduces you to why metal is such an attractive material to work with. You learn why I fell in love with metal in the first place. Then I share some practical information to get you started in your own metal experiences. I provide tips on choosing a location and a work surface. As your needs grow, you may need more space. I talk about those possibilities as well. Finally, I talk about safety in the studio. With a few precautions, you can keep yourself and your space safe, too.

Appreciate Metal's Appeal

When I first worked with metal, I had never been exposed to a material that behaved like it did. My mother works with fabric. My father, wood. No one in my world had worked with metal. I had no frame of reference for its many wonders.

Soon, metal became an obsession. I couldn't learn about it fast enough. I could cut it with a tiny saw blade, heat it, smash it with a hammer, bend it, and unify two pieces. I could do that over and over. In the end, I had a piece of jewelry that was nice to look at and strong enough to be worn every day. That pleased me. I fell in love with the plastic qualities of metal and have never looked back.

You'll have your own reasons for working with metal. It offers a world of possibilities. You can boss it around, and it obeys. When you shape, bend, and stretch it, those efforts stay in its memory until you want it to do something else. You can embellish it with gemstones, other metals, twigs, and plastics, to name a few. You can color it in many ways. It's valued for its preciousness. You can use it create jewelry that lives for generations. Those qualities and more make for a pretty powerful magnet. It has drawn craftspeople, just like you, to working with metal for hundreds of years.

Choose Your Place

Even on a budget and in a tight space, a good metalsmithing setup has some key features. When selecting a workspace, look for and consider these things:

Work surface. You'll need a solid work surface of some type. It's important to use a surface that can withstand some hammering without bouncing around.

Good lighting. This can be overhead lighting. You also can clamp additional lighting to your work surface as a supplement.

SAFE 'SMITHING

Clip-on fans with absorbent charcoal filters are meant for low-temperature circuit-board soldering. I don't recommend these for silver soldering or other fume-producing activities. The surface of the charcoal becomes saturated so quickly that it won't be of much use to you. A true HEPA filtration unit will help clean the air in your studio. It can't be relied upon, however, to draw fumes away from you at the soldering bench.

Electricity. Depending on the amount of power equipment you have, you'll need a certain number of outlets.

Air flow. Ventilation is imperative if you are soldering or working with chemical patinas. An open door, window, or fan blowing across your workspace is an option. Installing a kitchen vent fan is another possibility. You can also opt for self-contained equipment available from jewelry suppliers if you'll be soldering on a regular basis.

Water. If you won't have a sink in the area, you'll need to bring in a couple of containers. Sometimes you'll need to transport your work to a sink with running water for cleanup.

Safety equipment and features. You'll need the proper protective gear, storage for chemicals and gas tanks, and a fire extinguisher. You'll need to control access to the area when you are working with fire or chemicals.

Plan Your Space

Assuming that you will be using part of your living space for your metalwork, you may need to utilize multiple areas to get your jobs done. For example, you might set up a table in the corner of your garage to do most of your work, and then take items to be cleaned to your kitchen sink.

If you have a dedicated studio space, then you may be able to designate areas for specific tasks. For example, some metalsmiths solder right at their workbench.

To keep your interest up and frustration down, it pays to have an easy system of organization. Plan a workspace where all your tools and supplies are right where you need them when you need them.

Small workspaces tend to need the most careful consideration. You want a space that meets your requirements. Be sure your small space contains a sturdy work surface; a bench pin with clamp that attaches to your work surface; a place to stow your tools and supplies; good lighting; and a supportive, adjustable chair.

ARTISAN TIP

A workspace without any carpeting is good. Carpet gets dirty quickly, and hot items melt carpet fibers in an instant. A concrete floor is best. If it is painted one solid color, dropped items can be easily spotted.

This workspace has all the necessary elements for metalsmithing.

Having access to a larger workspace can make metalsmithing easier. However, your layout is still an important factor to consider. Once you've taken stock of your amenities, review your activities. Dedicate space for each major activity you will perform in the studio. For example, all work that requires heat or soldering takes place in one area. Activities that require power equipment can take place around locations with outlets.

Make sure children and pets can't access your stored metalworking supplies. Control access when you are actively working, too. Be aware of and take all proper measures to keep chemicals, tools, or flame sources away from kids, pets, and unknowing people.

An Easy Organization System

When organizing your workspace, look for ways to use what you already have. Repurposed trays and cookie sheets that can be stacked with your supplies are helpful. Low, flat storage containers with locking lids are great, too. You can stack these and stow them away on a shelf for easy retrieval when needed. If you can't find what you need at home, hardware stores sell lots of ways to store small parts that work great in a metalsmith's studio.

Use small trays and jars in groups to hold tools and equipment that perform similar tasks. For example, if you have lots of stamps, you can group them in containers that are placed in the same box or tray. When you need to perform a stamping operation, grab your tray.

Plan vertically. Pegboard and hooks make use of wall space. Overhead shelves don't take up room in the studio and work well for less-used items.

Labeling the contents of storage drawers, bins, and containers will save you lots of time. For safety's sake, be sure to label any containers of stored chemicals. These should be stored together, in a secure place away from other materials.

Find the Right Work Surface

If you are new to metalsmithing, the importance of a high-quality work surface may not be obvious. Once you've hammered or sawed metal, however, you will know why your work surface is so important. A stable work surface of solid wood at least one inch thick is best.

When you hammer metal on a flimsy or too-resilient surface, two things become clear. First, everything jumps around. Second, the work surface isn't able to absorb the excess energy directed at the metal. If there is no place for that energy to travel, it's going to go right back into your body. Your joints and muscles will absorb the shock, strain, and impact, and you will wear yourself out. Your body is your first tool. Your work surface is second. Make sure the second tool takes care of the first.

Workbench Features

A jeweler's or watchmaker's bench is designed specifically to handle the rigors of specialized metalsmithing tasks. Jeweler's benches often come with a sweeps drawer. Many come with a small slot in front to hold the bench pin so that you can position the bench pin more centrally over the *sweeps drawer* in order to preserve filings and other metal scraps. Jeweler's benches also have small drawers along one side to hold tools.

Instead of the jeweler's bench sweeps drawer, a watchmaker's bench has a cloth-lined catch tray to prevent tiny parts from bouncing if dropped. A watchmaker's catch tray is positioned higher than a jeweler's sweeps drawer because jewelers need clearance for their sawing movements. A watchmaker's bench also has a lip along the front edge to prevent parts or tools from rolling off. A watchmaker's bench is equipped with more drawers than a jeweler's bench, but it lacks a slot for the bench pin.

> **DEFINITION**
>
> A **sweeps drawer** is a pull-out tray for capturing metal shavings and dust.

When shopping for a bench, invest in the features you want the most. For example, some work benches come equipped with slide-out armrests. These offer places to support your arms.

After your bench arrives and you have set it up, test-drive it to make sure it is the right height. Pull your chair up to the bench. Adjust the chair so your knees are parallel with the floor. The working surface and bench pin should be at about breastbone height in order to keep your neck in a more neutral, forward-facing position. If you need to make adjustments, add height to your bench rather than raising or lowering your chair.

You can adjust the height of your workbench easily. I have two 2×4-inch boards spanning the legs of my workbench. One is under the left pair of legs and one is under the right pair of legs. This lifts the bench to the proper height for me.

Embellish your bench with nails, pegs, and hooks to hold the tools you use most often. I have three nails on the left side of my bench top to hang my three saw frames. A nail on the left leg holds a ring mandrel. The pedal of my flex shaft is nailed to the board on the right side of the bench. I changed out the bench pin that came with my bench and added a different one, screwing it to the bench to secure it. I added all of these treatments over time, as the need became apparent. Don't be afraid to modify your bench to suit your needs.

The Role of the Bench Pin

The bench pin is the whipping boy of the metalsmith's studio. It's meant to be used up. It is there to support your work while you are sawing. It steadies your work while you push, bend, and file against it. It holds tools to free up hands for other tasks. It is the wood into which drill bits go when they have passed through metal. Every metalsmith needs a bench pin.

The bench pin can be quickly modified to help make a bunch of tasks easier. Try these ideas to modify your bench pin:

- File or cut little notches in the front. You can use your jeweler's saw to make these cuts. This helps to steady rings and wire.

- Drill holes part or all the way through your bench pin. Match the drill bit to your favorite wire sizes.

- Dig a tiny ditch in the top with a knife or drill bit. This can hold tiny things you're working with such as gemstones or decorative elements.

ARTISAN TIP

To make your own bench pin, take a piece of hardwood about ½-inch (about 1 centimeter) thick, 6 inches (about 15 centimeters) long, and 3 or 4 inches (about 8 to 10 centimeters) wide. Cut a V shape in the front of one end of the wood. A good starting point is to begin the V shape about ½ inch from either side of the edges of the wood. The V comes to a point 2 inches (5 centimeters) inside the edge of the wood. Use a C-clamp to secure the bench pin to the front of your work surface.

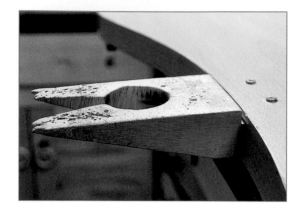

This bench pin has been screwed into the bench top.

The bench pin needs to be securely clamped to your work surface. Most work benches come with a slot that accepts the pin, but some don't. If you're using an alternative work surface, it won't have a slot. In these cases, you'll need to make one. You can fasten the bench pin using a C-clamp. Position the clamp on your nondominant side. Or you can screw the bench pin to your work surface. You'll lose the easy ability to quickly change the pin or flip it over to use the other side, but you'll gain a very stable surface. Consider screwing down the pin if a clamp doesn't cut it for you.

It's handy to have extra bench pins in other configurations. Some types have two sides, one angled and one straight. The straight side is face-up when you are holding metal for sawing or piercing. The angled side is face-up when you are propping work against it for sanding and filing. Other bench pins have a small, built-in anvil component. You can also make one yourself whenever you need it, with only a short length of hardwood.

Good Work Surfaces on a Budget

A good work surface is one that is strong and sturdy and doesn't bounce when you hammer on it. For example, an old desk with a wood top works great. Consider adding cross-bracing to wobbly desks or tables. Or place them against a wall. Position elements so that hammering and other actions requiring greater force take place over the leg of your table or desk. The leg helps absorb more of the force of your work.

This bench pin is clamped to a table.

If the top of your chosen work surface is thin, or isn't made from wood, you can modify it. Have a piece of wood cut to fit the entire top or a portion of the top. A butcher's block or several thinner boards glued together will give you the thickness you need. You can clamp or nail this to your original work surface.

Finally, if none of these are an option, simply take a bench pin and clamp it to whatever work surface is available to you. You'll have an instant workbench!

Play It Safe

You can be safe and have fun in your metalsmithing work by considering the following factors:

Ergonomics. Setting up your workbench at the proper height, taking stretch breaks, and using different muscle groups are important.

Eating. Keep food and drink away from any areas where they could become contaminated.

Labeling and MSDS Sheets. Adopt the habit of reading the label of everything that comes into your studio. Obtain Material Safety Data Sheet (MSDS) information from vendors or online.

Washing up. Clean your hands thoroughly throughout the day, especially when working with copper or nickel silver. If substances land on your skin or face, wash them off immediately.

Chemicals. Learn what you need to do to use, store, neutralize and dispose of chemicals that come into your workspace.

Organization. Take the time to organize your studio and keep it clean. Put things back as you use them.

To outfit your safe studio, you'll need these basic items:

- Eye protection—even if you wear glasses
- Hearing protection for long bouts of hammering
- Work apron to protect your skin and clothing
- Work gloves and rubber gloves to protect your hands from abrasions and chemicals
- Dust mask to protect your lungs from particulate matter
- Respirator to protect your lungs from caustic or poisonous fumes
- Well-stocked first aid kit that includes burn ointment
- ABC-rated fire extinguisher—position it between the exit and the torch

These essential supplies are part of your metalsmith's toolkit. Be prepared to have them in your studio. Always use them as needed.

CHAPTER 2

Choosing Tools and Equipment

In This Chapter

- A sound tool philosophy
- Tool checklists from the bare minimum to a happy medium and beyond
- Torch setups
- More advanced tools

This chapter focuses on tools. Oh, the multitude of choices! Fortunately, you only need a handful to begin making jewelry.

In this chapter, I give you several lists of tools you'll want to stock in your metalsmith toolbox. I explain all the tools in detail, including what each does and how to use the tool properly and safely. Finally, this chapter shows some basic torch setup plans and explains silver soldering.

My Tool Philosophy

When I first started down the gilded path of metal jewelry making, the tool options were overwhelming, and I wanted them all. Fortunately, I had a patient teacher who spent a good deal of time talking about tools and equipment and paging through supply catalogs with me. She got me to consider making some of my own tools, using tools I already had, and evaluating when to spend and when to save. (Thanks, Marilyn!)

Eventually I learned more about what I truly needed to bring my dreams to life in metal. I focused on building my knowledge base with intention and learning to use basic tools well. An increasingly complex set of techniques enabled me to advance.

Consider beginning with relatively few tools and using them well. As you learn best practices with your tools and get comfortable with them, the work you make will improve. As you desire to tackle other techniques, you may need to acquire a special tool or piece of equipment, but it isn't a given. New techniques don't automatically require the purchase of new tools. However, when frustration with the wrong tool for the job reaches a fever pitch, go for the right tool for the right job.

Source Tools Creatively

Review some of the techniques and projects in this book to see which ones you are most interested in trying, and take note of the tools required for each. Review the tools themselves and how to use them. Then look over the choices on your list and determine how you might be able to obtain that item or items without spending any money. For example, you could modify an existing tool or other object, try out tools in a workshop or school environment, purchase secondhand tools, trade or swap tools (look for local lapidary clubs or other groups), make your own tools, or borrow a tool from a fellow jewelry maker.

Know When to Spend and When to Save on Tools

Attend any class or workshop and fellow classmates will pass around their newest tool treasure to the pleasure, delight, and sometimes envy of others. Even metalsmiths who have been working for years can easily fall into the tool trap of "I've got to have that!" Don't feed the tool monster! You don't have to follow austerity measures—just take a commonsense approach to an expensive pastime. There will be a time where you simply must have the best tool. Be ready for it.

First, plan. For the following items, quality definitely matters:

Hand files and needle files. Buy cross-cut files, the best you can afford, in the shapes that will do the job you need done. Larger hands will be more comfortable holding larger sizes of files.

Scissors. You will use these to cut out paper patterns, labels, and fine wire and solder snippets. They should be sharp. My favorites are Joyce Chen kitchen shears.

Hand shears. These need to be able to cut nonferrous metal sheet and wire up to 18-gauge thick without leaving serrated marks to deal with.

Scribe. A good one made of tool steel will last a lifetime or more. Look for the type with two working ends. You can polish or "dress" the edges to suit you.

Metal-forming hammers. These include planishing, forging, and goldsmith's hammers. These move metal, and the mark they leave behind should please you and not require any additional cleanup effort. When you use a good hammer properly, sanding your work is unnecessary. Hammers should have well-polished steel faces; sturdy, well-balanced handles; and a good fit between the hammer head and handle—no wobbling.

You can spend less and save money on the following basic tools and still get a good value:

Saw frames	Steel stamps
Bench pins	Steel bench block
Dapping blocks or punches	Ball-peen hammer
Center punch (regular or spring-loaded automatic)	Brass hammer
	Rawhide mallet

Generally, I prefer to invest dollars in tools that perform more than one function. Then I look for high-grade, hardened steel hand tools that help me achieve or maintain a particular shape, such as a hand file or a well-polished forging hammer. Finally, tools that may get less use but need to perform a high-precision task are important in my hour of need: stone-setting punches, miter box, or parallel-action pliers.

The Tools You Need to Get Started

You probably already have some basic tools and supplies already:

- ❑ Permanent fine-tip and broad-tip markers
- ❑ Pencils
- ❑ Spiral notebook or sketchbook
- ❑ Fine-point scissors
- ❑ White stick-on labels
- ❑ Masking tape
- ❑ Double-stick tape
- ❑ Stainless-steel ruler with metric and inch marks
- ❑ Dawn dishwashing detergent
- ❑ Green scrubbing pad
- ❑ Wet/dry sandpaper in assorted grits
- ❑ Steel wool (000 grade, extra fine)
- ❑ Ball-peen hammer
- ❑ Center punch or nail
- ❑ Dividers with two pointed ends
- ❑ Fine-point tweezers

These items will help make up your first toolbox. As you progress, replace these items with proper metalworking tools more befitting your skill level and budget.

This list of tools and supplies will get you started with the bare-bones basics:

- ❑ Jeweler's saw, a dozen size 2/0 saw blades
- ❑ Cross-cut hand files: number 2 half-round file, number 2 flat file
- ❑ Cutters: small, flush-cut pliers and metal shears, aviation shears, or tinsnips
- ❑ Steel bench block or "found" steel, 3-inch (about 8 centimeters) square or larger
- ❑ Package of needle files (round, half round, square, triangle)
- ❑ Scribe
- ❑ Pliers: round, flat, and chain nose (buy as a set to save)
- ❑ Protective equipment: safety glasses, ear plugs, apron, work gloves, rubber gloves
- ❑ Bench pin with V-slot, clamp to attach to work surface
- ❑ Center punch
- ❑ Sharp nail (to make holes in metal)
- ❑ Ball-peen hammer (one flat end, one rounded end)
- ❑ Wet/dry sandpaper or emery paper in 220 or 320 and 400 or 500 grits
- ❑ Steel ruler with inches and millimeters
- ❑ Permanent marker, pencils, paper, peel-and-stick labels

To increase the number of projects that you can complete, add the following tools to the quick-start toolbox as needed:

- ❑ Bench vise
- ❑ Hand drill
- ❑ Set of small drill bits
- ❑ Dividers (with two pointed ends)
- ❑ Files: number 3 barrette file
- ❑ Magnification: reading glasses, binocular headband magnifier, or 10x jeweler's loupe
- ❑ Hammers: planishing, riveting, forging, rawhide mallet
- ❑ Templates: circles, ovals, squares, and rectangles in varying sizes
- ❑ Wood-dapping block and punches
- ❑ Sliding brass gauge
- ❑ Steel mandrel

ARTISAN TIP

Eventually, tools wear out. Then they are ready for their next life. For example, a sharp file, even with care, will eventually wear and filing action will dull. It can then be modified into a decorative punch, scraper, or used as a forming mandrel.

When you are ready for stone setting, slightly more advanced forging, forming, and precision measuring, check out this equipment: (check out the last section in this chapter, "Specialty Equipment," for details on these items):

- ❏ Flexible shaft machine and number 30 handpiece
- ❏ Bits and assorted specialty burs for the flexible shaft machine, including stone-setting burs in the proper sizes for your gemstones
- ❏ Anvil to meet or exceed the size of your work
- ❏ Stakes for use with anvil as needed
- ❏ Digital caliper
- ❏ Stone-setting tools: burnisher, bezel roller and pusher, length of horn or plastic for smoothing

Basic Torch Setups

Eventually, most metalsmiths and jewelry makers yearn for a torch. You can use a torch to solder, ball up the ends of wire, melt small amounts of metal, anneal metal to soften it, and apply a heat patina to your metal. Yet the prospect of actually purchasing, setting up, and using a torch safely can be daunting. To make the process easier, it's best to eliminate some of the more exotic setups from consideration and concentrate on a few approachable systems that will work for several applications. For reasons of simplicity and cost-effectiveness, recommendations for single-fuel torch setups dominate the conversation here.

The type of torch you will use in your own home or studio depends on what type of operations you want to accomplish, which will determine how hot your flame needs to burn. Finding out where you can get fuel refills also is important. Make sure you can buy fuel at a location near you.

The following section discusses five key types of torches. Two are considered general use torches and are available as all-in-one units. Two are specifically designed as jeweler's torches and are available with a tank or tanks and a handpiece with interchangeable tips. The last one is a larger plumber's torch setup, which is similar in design to a jeweler's torch.

All-in-One Torches

Butane and propane torches are two types of all-in-one or general purpose torches. They are low-cost, small, and easy to use for the home jewelry maker. They get hot, but not as hot as jeweler's torches. Their tanks are easy to refill or change. They are best for melting balls on the ends of wire, soldering on a small scale, annealing metal, and creating heat patinas. You also can

This Blazer mini-torch is one of the few butane torches you can use to anneal small amounts of metal and do small soldering jobs.

(Photo courtesy of Blazer Products)

find both butane and propane general-purpose torches at most big-box home improvement and hardware stores or online.

Butane torches have a temperature range of 2,000 to 2,500 degrees Fahrenheit (1,093 to 1,371 degrees Celsius). The average size is 6 inches (about 15 centimeters) or less. An integral spark igniter makes lighting them easy. Most have a removable base that allows you to sit the torch on a tabletop. Tank fuel typically lasts only 90 minutes. Use only triple-refined butane fuel (not "premium" fuel) for refills, and make sure the refill nozzle (or nipple) is compatible with your specific torch.

Propane torches range in temperature from 3,400 to 3,450 degrees Fahrenheit (1,871 to 1,899 degrees Celsius). Marketed mainly as a plumber's torch, a propane torch uses a 1-pound disposable tank. Bernz-o-Matic is the industry leader in small propane torches. I set up my first studio in my garage with this type of torch.

Propane torches are often available with a couple of varieties of handpieces. For example, one type connects directly to the top of the tank and has an integral spark igniter. You hold the entire unit in your nondominant hand while using. This makes it a bit unwieldy but still useable. The other type uses a length of hose to connect the tank to the torch handpiece. Newer styles have an integral igniter.

Propane torches offer several options for handpieces.

Note that the rather high pressure of the flame on these options can be tricky to manage with delicate soldering operations. It can blow bits of metal and solder out of place.

Jeweler's Torches

Jeweler's torches are, of course, made specifically for jewelers' use. There are two different types. The first is fuel mixed with ambient air, known as fuel/ambient air or fuel/atmospheric torches. The second type is fuel mixed with oxygen from a tank, known as fuel/oxygen torches.

Each jeweler's torch system offers a fuel source (tank or tanks) and a separate handpiece connected by a hose, with a regulator in between. Each handpiece offers different tips. You can change them out to get different flame sizes. The torch has a knob or pair of knobs to adjust the intensity of the flame.

There are several types of torch fuels, but acetylene and propane are the most readily available and approachable. Both acetylene and propane are available in larger, refillable tanks. The most common tank size is a B tank, which is 23 inches (58 centimeters) tall and weighs 23 pounds (10 kilograms). This size and larger size tanks should always be used in the upright position and secured to the wall or leg of a table with a chain, or placed in an appropriate cart. Many tanks are equipped with a knob to turn the gas on or off. Some are not so equipped and require a valve wrench. Always leave the valve wrench on the valve in case the gas needs to be shut off quickly. Propane also is available in 1-pound (454-gram) disposable tanks (usually painted yellow) to pair with oxygen in 1-pound (454-gram) disposable tanks (usually painted green).

Each of these torch systems requires a striker to create a spark to start the flame. Never use an open flame, such as from a cigarette lighter or another torch, to light a torch.

A fuel/ambient air torch with acetylene fuel has a temperature of 4,220 degrees Fahrenheit (2,327 degrees Celsius). The tank is refillable. You need only one tank with a fuel-atmospheric torch setup, one regulator, and a handpiece. This torch is hot enough for all soldering operations in the studio and will melt small amounts of scrap metal. Respected winners in this category are the Silver Smith and Prest-o-Lite torches.

A fuel/oxygen torch with propane fuel has a temperature of 5,111 degrees Fahrenheit (2,822 degrees Celsius). It is available for use with disposable tanks and larger, refillable tanks. You need two of everything (except the handpiece) with fuel-oxygen torches: two tanks, two sets of regulators, two sets of flashback arrestors, and a torch handpiece. Propane doesn't get hot enough to warrant the upgraded system until it is mixed with oxygen, making it the hottest-burning torch of the group. And it's probably more torch than the average user will require. Respected winners in this category are the Smith Little Torch and Gentec Small Torch.

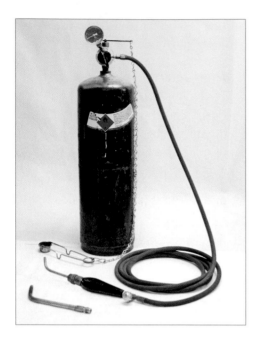

A plumber's torch setup includes a regulator, tank, and handpiece.

DEFINITION

Flux is a paste or liquid applied to metal to prevent oxidization and aid the flow of solder during soldering operations. Flux is available in many compositions, some of which are toxic. Read labels and ventilate your soldering area accordingly.

Plumber's Torch

A plumber's torch offers the same type of setup as the jeweler's torches. It contains a tank and a handpiece with a hose to connect them. It is lit using a striker. It is available in the same fuel types, either as a one-tank or two-tank system. The refillable tanks are available in the B size mentioned previously or larger sizes. They are often used in classrooms due to their low cost and durability. The main difference is that the handpieces available are larger and not as elegant for jewelry work as proper jeweler's torches. But they can be great for lots of annealing and all but the most delicate soldering projects. I still use one in my studio.

Torch Workstation Checklist

Chapter 8 details the ins and outs of using a torch to solder metal. For now, the following list will help you set up your soldering station:

- ❑ Your selected torch setup for soldering
- ❑ Heatproof soldering surface (for example, kiln bricks, Solderite pad, or ceramic honeycomb)
- ❑ Pickle warming pot or slow cooker with glass or plastic lid
- ❑ Two small containers, one for quenching with water, the other for a baking soda/water neutralizing bath
- ❑ Soldering pick (titanium pick or a piece of coat hanger wire sharpened on one end or the sharpened end of a graphite pencil)
- ❑ *Flux* (premade paste or liquid, such as Handy-Flux, Grifflux, Ultra Flux, Pripp's Liquid, or more expensive Firescoff, which doesn't require pickling to remove)

- ❏ Natural bristle *flux* brush (inexpensive artist's brush)
- ❏ Cross-lock and fine-point tweezers
- ❏ Pickle compound (sodium bisulphate, which is sold as Sparex; any pool cleaner; or the less-toxic Silver Prep by Cool Tools)
- ❏ Baking soda
- ❏ Copper or plastic tongs
- ❏ Fine-point scissors
- ❏ Hard, medium, and easy silver solders in either wire or sheet (not plumber's solder or brazing solder)
- ❏ Striker or torch lighter (not a cigarette lighter)
- ❏ Stainless steel T-pins
- ❏ Optional: charcoal block (in addition to heatproof soldering surface)
- ❏ Optional: a battery-operated spark igniter

You can use a slow cooker on the "low" setting to hold pickle solution (never let it boil). *Pickle* is a mild acid and water solution used to remove flux residue as well as oxides that are created when you use a torch to anneal or solder metal. When mixing your pickle solution, remember to always add acid to water—never add water to acid or you may cause the acid to spatter. Follow the directions that come with your pickle solution. To use pool cleaner as a pickle, add about a half a cup (118 milliliters) of cleaner to a gallon (3.75 liters) of water.

A pickle solution should last many months. Eventually, it will become saturated with copper particles, turning the solution a deep blue. Keep using your solution, occasionally adding water to it as needed, until it no longer works for you. Then neutralize it. Turn off the pot and allow it to cool. Add 1 teaspoon (5 milliliters) of baking soda to the pot. The solution will bubble violently. Once the bubbling dissipates, continue to add baking soda to the pot until no more bubbling occurs. Dispose of spent solution according to local regulations.

The lid on the pickle pot should be glass or plastic rather than metal. The warm pickle vapors collect on the lid of the crock pot over time and eventually cause the metal to rust.

> **ARTISAN TIP**
>
> A slow cooker works well to warm pickle solution. Over time, though, the glazing on the inside of the cooker can develop tiny cracks. Those cracks can allow the pickle solution to come into contact with the clay body of the cooker. Clay usually contains iron, which will react with the pickle solution to copper-plate everything in the cooker. When this happens, it is time to replace the cooker.

When that happens, the water droplets containing the rust will condense and drip down into the pickle pot, creating a contaminated pickle. You can prevent this type of contamination by replacing lids with metal trim with lids of plastic or glass. Also, keep the outside of your pickle pot wiped down to prevent it from corrosion due to dripping pickle solution.

Safe Torch Practices

This section highlights certain important safety precautions but is by no means an exhaustive list. Welding shops and fuel suppliers are a great resource for your torch and fuel needs. They will often help set up tanks with hoses, torch handpieces, and flashback arrestors upon request. They also will show you how to see what a gas leak looks like when leak-detection fluid is applied.

Fire extinguisher. Obtain a Class ABC dry chemical fire extinguisher for your studio. These multipurpose extinguishers are filled with mono ammonium phosphate, a nontoxic sticky yellow powder. They are available in several sizes. Read the instructions on the label before you need the extinguisher. Recharge all extinguishers after use, regardless of how much or little was used. Contact your local fire department for information about how to use and recharge fire extinguishers and general fire safety information.

Heat-resistant work surface. Line your work surface with heat-resistant cement backer board, a large ceramic tile, or a large baking pan.

Heatproof soldering surface. This item goes on top of or inside your heat-resistant work surface. Use a kiln brick, ceramic honeycomb block, charcoal block, pumice-filled turntable, Solderite pad, or soldering pad-filled turntable.

Leak-detection fluid. Use a leak-detection fluid on torches that have hoses and regulator valves to check for bubbles, which indicate leaks. If you see bubbles, retighten all connections. If bubbles still occur, take your torch back to the location where it was filled and obtain assistance. You should use Safe-D-Tect, Windex, soapy water, or other leak-detection liquid weekly whenever tanks are changed out. You won't need this fluid with small, butane, handheld torches.

> **SAFE 'SMITHING**
>
> Don't buy shiny, new, expensive tanks for refills. Most suppliers that provide tank refills simply swap empty tanks with full ones. That means kissing your shiny new tanks goodbye the first time you fill them up. Instead take your torch handpiece with you the first time you need a tank or tanks, and discuss renting or purchasing tanks directly from your supplier. Many fuel suppliers will deliver and swap out tanks for you. If you transport your own tanks, keep them upright and strapped in the back of an open pickup truck. Empty or full, tanks are dangerous in the event of an accident.

Ventilation. An overhead ventilation system or an open window or door with a fan blowing across your work surface as you solder will help carry fumes away.

Flashback arrestors. These devises attach to hose lines near the fuel tanks of larger setups between the tank and the handpiece. They prevent the flame from burning back to the tank. These are often employed on plumber's torches and welding setups. Sometimes these are part of a torch kit, but they often need to be purchased separately. If they are not included with your setup, be sure to purchase them.

Welding glasses. You need these when using a propane/oxygen or acetylene/oxygen torch setup.

Hair ties or clips. If you have long hair, make sure that it is tied or clipped back from your face as you solder.

Flammable items. Remove all paper and other flammable items from the soldering area.

I highly recommend getting expert guidance in setting up a larger torch in your home or studio for the first time, even if you have used torch setups in a school or classroom situation. The smaller, handheld butane torches are a bit more approachable on your own.

Specialty Equipment

When you're ready for specialty equipment, this is the section for you. Most complete metalsmithing studios will contain the popular items described in this section.

Flexible shaft machine. A flexible shaft machine consists of a hanging motor with a spinning, rubber-sheathed shaft that powers a small handpiece. A variety of handpieces are available for flexible shaft machines. Number 30 is a commonly used handpiece. It sports an adjustable chuck that accepts burs and drill bits of different sizes and types. A good flexible shaft machine can last a lifetime with care. You can find many quality models for under $200, and lower-horsepower versions are available for less than $100. Be sure to run your flexible shaft machine at the slowest speed possible to do the job.

A flexible shaft machine is one of the first big purchases I made as a metalsmith, and I've never regretted it. A foot pedal (not shown) is needed to operate the machine.

ARTISAN TIP

Flexible shaft machines are commonly offered in packaged kits containing the motor, a handpiece, foot pedal, and an assortment of burs. These may seem like a good value, but you may end up using only a few of the burs. I recommend buying the machine and foot pedal and a number 30 adjustable chuck handpiece. Then purchase specific burs to do the jobs you want to do. I also recommend *Making the Most of Your Flex-shaft* by Karen Christians (MJSA Press, 2005).

Burs. If you get a flexible shaft machine, you will want a variety of drill burs. For example, crazy hairs (3M radial bristle discs) in various grits are good for polishing. Cup burs in 1- to 3-millimeter sizes are useful for smoothing the ends of earwires and small decorative metal balls.

If you want to create your own tube settings so you can set round, faceted gemstones, you'll need stone-setting burs. These burs are used to cut a seat into tubing in the exact dimension of your gemstone. The setting bur needs to be the same dimension, or just slightly smaller, than your stone. Burs cut a path slightly larger than the bur. Try 2- to 3-millimeter gemstones to begin. Don't exceed 4- to 5-millimeter gemstones.

Bud burs, ball burs, flame burs, and Krause burs all cut into metal and can create decorative divots upon which you can build interesting designs and patterns. Choose the size that suits your design needs.

Bits. You will need drill bits matched to the size of holes you would like to make. When in doubt, use a drill bit slightly smaller than the hole you want, because the bit makes a slightly larger cut than its actual size. Also, you can make a small hole bigger.

Always use a lubricant on burs or drill bits. Remember to slowly begin the rotation of any bur or bit before you apply it to the metal. Stop the rotation after you have removed the bur or bit from the metal. Keep a slow, steady pace as you go. This will keep your progress moving smoothly and prevent the bur from overheating, getting bound up in metal, or being damaged.

Rolling mill. A rolling mill is used to roll metal into thinner gauges of sheet and wire. It is also widely used in a technique known as roller printing, in which you use texture plates, sheets of paper, fabrics, string, wire, or organic materials to add texture to annealed metal. Some rolling mills come with integral texture rollers. Some machines are equipped with a combination roller, which means both wire and sheet surfaces share the same roller. These machines are available with hand cranks for the jeweler's studio. Motorized machines are found in industrial settings or production studios. Be sure your unit has solid, hardened steel rollers rather than hollow rollers. Hollow rollers are not as robust.

Anvil. You can find many sizes, shapes, and weights in hardened steel and iron anvils. A length of polished railroad tie makes an adequate anvil for the beginning jewelry maker. But if your jewelry making takes you into foldforming operations, general forging, and small-object making, look for an anvil that offers weight in the 35- to 50-pound range (16 to 23 kilograms); a horn (look for a long, tapered point) on one end and a squared area at the rear, also known as the London shape; a square hole called a Hardie hole in the rear of the anvil into which stakes can be set; and hardened steel polished to near-mirror finish.

Anvils need to be secured to a very heavy wood surface to keep them from moving while in use. Many metalsmiths attach anvils to tree stumps using small wood blocks nailed to the stump to snug up against the base of the anvil, or copper strips strapped over the base.

You can find used anvils through diligent searching. Good ones will come with no rust and still will cost a pretty penny, from around $3 to $5 per pound or more, close to the cost for a new one. Some anvils are worth redressing with an angle grinder and then sanding down to a 400-grit polish.

A good rolling mill is a true investment. Low-cost machines are available for around $200, but these cannot offer the precision or effortless gear operation of a higher-priced unit.

Hammers. If you need an anvil, be sure to use well-polished hammers to complement it. For foldforming and forging operations, I use a 1,000-gram (2.2-pound) forging hammer with a hickory handle and a highly polished head. I use this hammer to create the most delicate surface texture on metal or to forge thick copper into sculptural shapes. One end of the head is flat and the other end is tapered to a broad, wide point.

Other valuable shapes are the planishing and forming hammers. A planishing hammer has two flat, polished surfaces. The flat surfaces are slightly domed. You use them to harden metal and smooth hammer marks. A forming hammer has two rounded heads. You use these to spread metal and to create a decorative hammer texture. You can also find a half-forming and half-planishing hammer, with one flat side and one round side. You can use any of these hammers with an anvil or a small steel bench block. Always keep some metal between your hammer and your steel-hitting surface.

Understanding Metal Materials

In This Chapter

- My materials philosophy
- The differences between various types of metal
- The basics of annealing and work hardening
- Tips on reusing metals

Metal offers unparalleled opportunities as a landscape for design. But in order to get good results in jewelry making, you need to understand some basics regarding the properties of metal. Metals need certain preparations before and during their use in jewelry making. This chapter explains what those preparations are and how you can do them.

Metals are precious. This chapter describes how to reuse and recycle your materials and a little bit about the refining process. You may eventually want to recycle existing jewelry, use some scrap metal you run across, or melt something down. I help you identify what you have and determine safe and simple ways to use it in your work.

Knowing Your Materials

A personal guiding light of my existence is frugality. My mother's mother was raised by immigrant parents and was widowed during the Great Depression. Oleta helped forge frugality in her children and granddaughters. So I'm all about making something beautiful with very few ingredients, whether it's dinner or jewelry.

This spirit applies to my approach to the raw materials themselves. I look for low-cost metals such as copper, brass, and even aluminum to complement more precious metals, such as silver and gold.

As you develop your practice, I encourage you to consider using as few tools as possible and really get to know your metal. Practice techniques in less expensive brass and copper first, but realize that you won't truly be able to develop skills as a metalsmith until you work with several metals. That often means investing in some more expensive metals.

I was fortunate in the beginning of my foray into metalsmithing that the price of silver hovered around $4 to $5 per troy ounce. (This is known as the spot price, and it changes on a daily basis.) I appreciate that I was able to continue experimenting early in my career with expensive materials such as silver and gold. I encourage you to do the same. Only then will you fully understand how each metal has its own properties and responds differently to sawing, bending, hammering, heating, and soldering. The secret is that the more precious the metal, the easier it is to work with—usually.

So invest in an array of metals, from low-cost-base metals to the more pricey sterling silver and even gold. Use minimal tools in the beginning. Learn about your metal. This is my philosophy, and I hope you'll give it a try.

Defining Metal Types and Properties

It pays to understand a bit about the makeup and characteristics of metals as a basis for your work. Although there are many types of metal, all metal shares these properties:

- Metals are a crystalline structure.

- Metals have high amounts of conductivity, meaning that they transport electrical energy and heat easily. Silver is the most conductive metal in the periodic table of elements.

- Metals are malleable, meaning they can bent and shaped.

- Metals are ductile, meaning they can be stretched certain amounts before breaking.

Metals are either ferrous, meaning they contain iron, or nonferrous, meaning they do not contain iron. Most jewelers use nonferrous metals.

Metals also are classified as precious metals or base metals. Examples of precious metals often used in jewelry making are gold, silver, and platinum. Precious metals are more rare and costly than base metals. Precious metals, such as silver and gold, are always sold by *troy weight*.

Base metals often used in jewelry making are copper, brass, nickel, and aluminum. Copper, in fact, was the first metal that humans discovered and used. Base metals are more abundant and less expensive than precious metals. Base metals are sold in various ways, such as by the sheet, coil, piece, or pound.

> **DEFINITION**
>
> **Troy weight** is a system of measurement for precious metals such as gold and silver. The troy ounce is different from the system of measurement Americans typically use, the avoirdupois ounce. One troy ounce equals 1.097 avoirdupois ounces.

Two or more metals melted together combine to form an alloy. The metals used most often in jewelry making are alloys. Each alloy has varying working properties, such as how malleable or ductile it is. Other important properties include annealing and melting temperatures. You'll learn more about these properties as you learn how to anneal and solder metals.

The metals that are used most often in jewelry making are various alloys of brass, Nu-Gold, copper, sterling silver, gold, and elemental platinum and palladium. Some of these metals can be used in their pure, elemental form, but they generally are found alloyed with at least one other metal to create a specific color or working property. There are literally hundreds of alloys. A few with great color and working properties are Argentium Sterling Silver (which is sterling silver with a small amount of germanium), Palladium white gold, and Palladium sterling silver. These metals are worthy of future attention and research. This book focuses mostly on the reasonably priced and readily available alloys of brass, Nu-Gold, copper, and sterling silver.

Preparing Your Metal

Metal is plastic. One of the elemental aspects of metal is its malleability and ductility. These properties allow metal to be formed and stretched and for the work to hold its shape. The plastic qualities of metal are what hooked me and keep me interested in working with this delightful material.

Before you can work metal properly, you must know how to prepare it so it will do your bidding. Two of these key processes are *annealing*, or softening metal, and *work hardening*, or toughening the metal.

DEFINITION

To anneal is to heat, then cool. **Annealing** softens the crystal structure of metal and allows you to move it more easily. To work-harden is to stiffen metal. **Work hardening** occurs during many metalsmithing processes, such as hammering, stamping, or generally working with metal sheet or wire in any way that exerts force.

Here are a few details about the metals that this book discusses:

Common Jewelry-Making Metals and Their Properties

Metal	Alloy Composition	Melt Point	Annealing Information
Brass	Copper and zinc	1,630 to 1,935°F* 888 to 1,057°C	Heat to bright orange red; air-cool
Bronze	Copper and tin	1,920 to 2,250°F 1,049 to 1,232°C	Heat to medium red; quench when black
Copper	Element	1,981°F* 1,083°C	Heat to dull red; quench when black
Gold	Element	1,945°F 1,063°C	Heat to dull red; quench when redness disappears
Nu-Gold	Copper and zinc	1,750°F* 954°C	Heat to bright red; air-cool
Silver	Element	1,761°F 961°C	Heat to dull red; quench when black
Sterling silver	Silver and copper	1,640°F 893°C	Heat to dull red; quench when black

Different alloys anneal at greatly varying temperatures.

There are no hard and fast rules for the annealing and melting points for alloys, unless you are able to determine exactly what the alloy consists of. This information is usually available from the vendor. If you are using scrap metal, you will need to be more careful. Don't melt any metal if you don't know what's in it!

ARTISAN TIP

Don't anneal metal before sawing it with a jeweler's saw. If you do, the metal will be too soft, and the saw blade will grab the softened metal and bend it rather than cutting through it. Instead, make sure metal is as flat as possible before sawing it, work hardening it when needed. Stiff metal is easier to saw than soft metal.

Annealing Metal

You have probably experienced bending a wire back and forth repeatedly until it breaks. The same properties apply to metal. If you exert force onto metal over and over again, it will break from the stress. You don't want that.

Before bending, shaping, stamping, or hammering your metal, anneal it. Annealing keeps metal from splitting or fracturing while you are working with it. Once metal is annealed, it remains annealed until force is exerted upon it.

The approach to annealing outlined here is easy and straightforward to do, but it varies with what type of metal you use. Follow these steps:

1. Prepare your torch station. Have torch, striker if needed, heatproof surface, ventilation, safety gear, tongs, pickle pot, baking soda and water mixture, and plain water at your station. See the "Basic Torch Setups" section in Chapter 2 for more information.

You need a torch and a heatproof surface to anneal metal.

2. Prepare your metal. Cut any sheets of metal you wish to anneal into the sizes you can manage. To anneal wire, wrap it into a coil and secure the coil by wrapping the end of the coil around itself to make a tight bundle. Or you can twist small pieces of iron binding wire around the coil to hold the metal. Keeping the wires you want to anneal bundled this way will prevent stray pieces from melting. Remove any binding wire before pickling.

3. Place your metal sheet or coiled wire on your heatproof surface. If possible, set metal sheets on a wire screen, iron wire nest, or broken pieces of heatproof blocks to allow the heat to travel underneath. You can also put everything in a heatproof pan on a turntable filled with pumice.

4. Heat the metal to the proper temperature. Point the flame of the torch straight down at the metal. Using the part of the flame that is just outside of the deep blue cone, you need to keep the flame moving until the metal glows a dull red for sterling silver or copper or an orange-red for brass. Watch for the color change as you move the flame across the metal's surface. This change might be easier to notice if the room is darkened.

The annealing setup on the left uses a pumice-filled pan sitting on top of a Solderite pad and enclosed by kiln bricks. The annealing setup on the right uses a wire grid sitting on top of a Solderite pad and enclosed by kiln bricks.

ARTISAN TIP

A trick to help indicate annealing temperature is to mark your metal with a black permanent marker. When the mark disappears, metal is annealed. You can also use a dot of liquid or paste flux applied to metal. When the flux bubbles and turns clear, the metal is annealed. These techniques work on copper, brass, sterling silver, and gold.

5. Air-cool or quench the metal. In the case of copper, you can quench the metal in water immediately. For sterling silver or other silver alloys, allow the red glow to disappear. This condition is called black heat. Then quench the metal in water. For brass, bronze, or nickel silver, allow the metal to air-cool. To bring the heat down fast when air-cooling these metals, place the metal on a piece of steel. If you try to quench them in water, they may shatter.

The photograph on the left shows blackened annealed metal before quenching. The photograph on the right shows annealed metal after quenching.

6. Pickle the metal. If desired, you can place the annealed metal in a warm pickle solution for about five minutes to remove the oxides created by the torch.

7. Neutralize and rinse the metal. Remove metal from the pickle pot using copper tongs. Swish it around for two or three seconds in a baking soda and water bath, and then rinse it with clean water.

8. Dry the metal with a hand towel or paper towel, removing all moisture before you introduce tools to your metal.

> **SAFE 'SMITHING**
>
> Never quench hot metal in the pickle pot! Hot acid can spew, burning you or those nearby. Always air-cool or quench metal in water before placing it in the pickle pot.

This piece of copper is being pickled.

To get metal really clean after pickling it, you can scrub it with a brass brush and soapy water.

Until you're familiar with annealing temperatures, you may want to dim the lights and watch for the metal to glow when you are heating it with the torch. Every section of the metal does not need to glow all at the same time as long as each section of the metal reaches proper temperature at some point during the annealing process.

Here are a few additional annealing tips:

- Every time you perform a soldering operation, your metal will be annealed.

- Air-cooling long or flat pieces of metal prevents them from warping upon being plunged into cold water.

- A steel wok filled two thirds of the way with pumice makes a great annealing pan. Don't use one with Teflon or other nonstick coatings.

- If you anneal thick metal or wire before cutting with hand shears, it will cut more easily.

- When making rivets, anneal the wire or tubing after cutting the lengths you need.

Familiarity with the properties and behaviors of metals and alloys can be a little-understood aspect of this craft. Knowing why metal needs to be softened before working with it and how to go about it will provide you with a good basis for comprehending much that goes into metalsmithing. Eventually, you'll realize that knowing these things will give you answers to questions you haven't even thought up yet.

Work-Hardening Metal

Just as annealing is critical to making metal do your bidding, so it goes with work hardening. It is helpful to have finished jewelry in a work-hardened state, because you want to wear jewelry such as earrings and bracelets without them bending out of shape.

Work hardening is often necessary during jewelry-making processes, too. It is easier to saw work-hardened metal, especially if you have an intricate pattern to cut. Otherwise, it's like sawing a marshmallow with a baseball bat. Work hardening also helps to stabilize the metal for filing operations. In general, you need to work-harden your metal when it bends too much during metalworking activities.

You harden metal by applying force or pressure to it through bending, twisting, pulling, or compressing. This force or pressure causes movement within the crystal structure of the metal. Hammering, twisting, stretching, and tumbling are all methods of work hardening.

You can work-harden your metal using any type of smooth-faced hammer, including rawhide or plastic mallets. Follow these steps:

1. Place your metal on a smooth wood or steel surface. Note that any texture or dents on your work surface will transfer to your metal.

2. Tap the metal with the smooth face of your hammer or mallet, overlapping each tap.

3. See, feel, and listen to the metal. You will begin to feel the metal move less the more you hammer. It will begin to sound different. Use your hands to bend and flex the metal slightly to check whether it is work-hardened enough for your purposes.

Twisting work-hardens metal sheet and wire. This action is often a byproduct of working with metal, but can also be put to good use to stiffen lengths of wire, create a decorative feature with square wire, and work-harden strips of metal. For wire, clamp or grasp about one quarter to one half of an inch in the jaws of two pairs of pliers or one pair of pliers and a vice. Gently twist the metal while also pulling the metal until it reaches your desired degree of work hardening. For strips of metal, use the same approach, except go very slowly to keep the metal from collapsing. Use your fingers to smooth and coax bends and twists.

ARTISAN TIP

Twisting is a good way to work-harden the post portion of post-style earrings. Once the post has been soldered to the earring, it will be soft. To harden it, hold the earring in one hand and grip about one-quarter inch of the post in a pair of pliers. Using pliers with serrated jaws can be helpful. Hold the wire taught and twist the pliers one full turn.

This silver wire has been work-hardened through twisting.

Stretching out a length of wire and pulling it taught will work-harden it. To do this, place about one-half inch (a little more than a centimeter) of wire in a vice. Keep the wire straight with no bends or kinks. Place the other end of the wire in a pair of serrated-jaw pliers. Give the pliers a few sharp, straight tugs to both straighten and work-harden the wire.

Using a barrel or rotary tumbler filled with polished steel or stainless steel shot will effectively work-harden metal. To tumble jewelry items, follow these steps:

1. Fill the barrel of the tumbler to half full with steel or stainless steel shot. Don't load the barrel with more weight than the stated capacity or it will not turn. If the barrel "jumps" while turning, try adding more stainless steel shot to stabilize it.

2. Add enough water and a burnishing compound to just cover the steel shot. I use a compound at about half of the recommended strength to cut down on froth. You can use a drop of dish detergent, but it creates a lot of bubbles.

3. Close the tumbler, and turn it on. Let it run for at least 1 hour and up to 24 hours. Personal preference will tell you how long to leave items in the tumbler.

4. Pour contents of the tumbler into a sieve placed over a bowl to capture the contents of the tumbler.

5. Rinse the contents and remove jewelry items. Discard the dirty water from the tumbler.

Jewelry and stainless steel shot are ready to tumble.

The tumbling action of a rotating barrel containing many small pieces of steel will harden and burnish jewelry without deforming it. This action also removes tarnish, but it can remove delicate surface textures and patinas from metal, too.

Recycling Metal

Metalsmiths have practiced recycling since the dawn of the craft. All scraps, mistakes, and even dust collected from sawing can be saved and reused in a variety of ways. Old jewelry and nonjewelry items also can be upcycled into fresh wearable creations.

Saving Your Scrap

At the bench, you can save your scrap using a number of methods. For example, you can use a sweeps catch. Attach one edge of a piece of leather under your bench or work surface, and place the free edge in your lap. This will capture dust and bits of metal and other small items that roll off of your work surface. A sweeps catch is especially helpful when you're working with gemstones.

> **SAFE 'SMITHING**
>
> Be sure to quench your charcoal block in water after every use. It stays hot for a long time. Dunking your block in water will prevent it from smoldering unattended and also prolong its useful life.

Some find it more convenient to work with a tray to collect sweeps. A sweeps tray can be the lower drawer in your bench. I place a cookie sheet in my drawer and brush the dust and bits of metal into a plastic bag in between projects. You could also place a cookie sheet in your lap. Just remember to remove it before standing up!

A key practice to adopt when recycling your metal scraps is to keep different types of metal separated at all times. Dropping bits of scrap into dedicated containers as you work is much easier than spending time painstakingly separating multiple types of metal from a single catch-all scrap container.

I keep small boxes near my workbench, one for each type of metal I'm working with. When I have scrap that's larger than dust, it goes into the appropriate scrap bin. To take it a step further, I keep separate containers for large pieces of scrap and small pieces of scrap. This way, I can quickly grab a scrap when I want to test-drive a stamp design or hammer texture.

Reusing Scrap

Once you have a collection of scrap, you can put it to use again. You can sell it, melt it, or use it for practice.

If you have silver or gold scrap, you can send it to a reputable refiner for a check or a purchase credit. I prefer to use refiners that provide evidence of utilizing green practices. Each refiner has certain procedures that you will need to follow. In general, you will want to make sure your precious metal scrap is separated by type, all solder is cut out, and gemstones are removed. A small postal scale can help you in determining an estimated weight. Multiply the postal scale ounce weight (avoirdupois) by .9114 to obtain troy ounce weight. See Appendix B for conversion factors.

If you have a torch setup, you can melt down small amounts of scrap for reuse. For example, you can melt silver or gold to create small spheres to use as decorative elements in many jewelry projects. Follow these steps:

1. Make small, round indentations in the surface of a charcoal block with the tip of a knife. Place very small amounts of scrap into these divots.

2. Heat the scrap with a torch until the metal gathers up and forms a ball. Move from area to area until all melting is complete.

3. Allow the balls to cool. The balls should be pretty clean because charcoal creates an environment where oxides are slow to form.

You may usually solder the balls to your work without having to pickle them first, even if they appear off-color.

For brass and copper, use the small scrap for small elements to solder onto the surface of the same metal or different metals. Keep some of the larger pieces to practice hammer techniques and test stamps and punches.

The high melting point of copper (1,981°F/1,083°C) makes it difficult to melt large amounts in the small studio. You can still melt the ends of wire using a torch or melt small bits of copper using good ventilation along with the technique described for melting silver and gold in this section.

SAFE 'SMITHING

Metal fume fever is caused by exposure to fumes from melting hefty amounts of zinc, copper, magnesium, or brass. It's a common occupational hazard of welders. Jewelry makers are susceptible to this illness, too. Flulike symptoms can last for a few hours, up to 24 hours. If you are melting metal scraps and notice a sweet or odd taste in your mouth, throat irritation, and coughing, stop immediately and get to fresh air.

Designing Jewelry

In This Chapter

- Elements of good design
- Idea sketches and sources of inspiration
- Steps for making paper models
- Factors to consider about your jewelry designs
- An important way to save time in the studio

Design is key in jewelry making. Consider it a prong of the jeweler's setting. Tools, materials, and techniques make up the first three prongs, and the fourth is good design. Without it, you have a bunch of techniques sitting there with nothing to say.

This chapter focuses on the basics of designing jewelry. It gets you to think about putting your dreams on paper before fabricating them from metal. My goal is to help you to find your own voice, so I discuss how to gather inspiration, pin your ideas to paper by adopting a sketchbook habit, and then take your sketches and create practical models. Things to think about when your design is ready to be launched are covered here, too.

Dreaming in Metal

The key elements all visual artists use also apply to good jewelry design. Artistic works possess a sense of unity. Even in asymmetrical designs, individual parts help balance the whole picture. A focal point draws the eye. Contrast and varying colors or textures are present, creating interest and movement. Good jewelry design contains these same elements.

In addition, jewelry complements the architecture of the human body. You want to make jewelry to wear or to give, presumably. So you must think of the landscape upon which your little work of art will come to rest. Wearability is the final key in good design.

You may already have some ideas about the jewelry you'd like to design and make. That's great. I put this design chapter fairly early in the book so that you can practice thinking about your design as you read about techniques in Part 2.

Recording Design Ideas and Finding Inspiration

You'll want a system to record design ideas and inspirations. Without a system for recording your inspirations, you will lose them forever. This system can be simple. Mine is. I record things in three ways: a night stand notebook, a journal, and a main sketchbook.

Some of my best designs have come to me in my dreams. There is openness in the nearly asleep mind that gets pushed aside in the hectic activities of the day. Something creative can show up in that in-between state. The little notebook by my bed is for these situations.

When an idea comes to me just before I fall asleep or awaken, I pin it down in my notebook before it dissolves.

I have been keeping a journal on and off for about four years. If I get an idea or a concept anytime, I'll write about it in my journal. The journal goes with me to business meetings. On the cover is the date I started and finished writing in it.

I keep my main sketchbook in my studio. It contains all of my design ideas, including drawings for clients. Even if the germ of the idea began in the notebook at home or on a scrap of paper, I transfer it to the main sketchbook. I write the day I started and finished the sketchbook on the cover.

I can easily take any of these parts of the system with me when I travel. Over the years, I have become devoted to this system. When I fail to use it, I become disorganized. You can honor your creativity by developing a system of your own. Do this by paying attention to your own ideas and dreams and find a way to record them. It will serve you well.

Once you have your main sketchbook, you'll want to start filling it up with inspiration. Grab a pen or a pencil and start looking. Design is all around us, every day. Simply choose to see things, and then record what you like in your sketchbook.

When making a quick sketch isn't an option, whip out your phone. Most have cameras these days. When you are back at a resting place, review the items you've photographed. Draw them in your book. Add your own notes and date them.

You can use tracing paper to expand upon your designs. Take an original drawing from your sketchbook, lay tracing paper over it, and draw other options. This method makes it easy to see where the design goes. The bonus? You still have your original design. Cut out and tape the tracing paper options next to your original design in your main sketchbook. Tracing paper also is useful in working out the details of your design, as explained in the next section.

> **ARTISAN TIP**
>
> Stuck? Think in threes. Try drawing simple sketches of just three elements from among your design options. An element can be anything: a texture, a color, a shape. Use this easy formula to start designing.

Using Paper Models to Work Out Your Design

Suppose you have an idea to make a pair of earrings by loosely twisting a strip of metal. You want the earrings to be long, dangly, and open. How long does your metal need to be? How many times should you twist the metal? An easy approach to this dilemma is to create a paper model. A model can be helpful in thinking through a dimensional design.

To make a paper model, you'll need these supplies:

Number 2 or HB pencil   Tracing paper

Sketchbook   Sharp scissors

To make the tracing paper model, follow these steps:

1. Draw your pattern for your model on your sketchbook using pencil. If you are making twisted earrings, for example, you need to know what the design looks like untwisted in order to have a pattern that can be applied to metal and cut out.

2. Take your tracing paper and lay it over your sketchbook, and use pencil to trace the outline of the image you just drew.

3. Cut the image out of tracing paper.

4. Turn and manipulate the model as needed.

5. If the paper is not the right size to do what you want, lay the tracing paper on your sketchbook again, adjusting your original drawing as needed. Repeat this step until you have a design on tracing paper that works.

6. Transfer the tracing paper design to your sketchbook. You now have a permanent drawing of the correct size model for future reference.

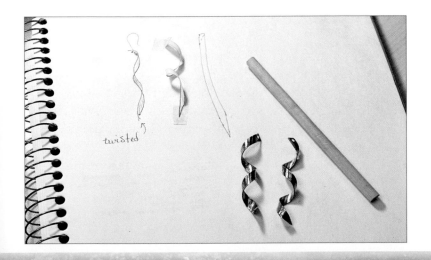

The paper model becomes the pattern for metal samples.

If the tracing paper isn't heavy enough to withstand manipulation, you can make a model using carbon paper, and then transfer the design to heavier paper.

To make a more heavyweight model, you'll need these supplies:

Number 2 pencil	Sharp scissors
Sketchbook	Light card stock or manila file folder
Tracing paper	Carbon paper

Follow these steps:

1. Place the page of your sketchbook on a hard surface.

2. Slide a piece of carbon paper under the area of the drawing, and place the card stock under the carbon paper.

3. Use a number 2 pencil to draw over your original drawing. If you are concerned about damaging your original drawing, place tracing paper over it. Then press down, following the lines of the original drawing.

4. Check your card stock to see if the transfer came through. Use the pencil to fill in lines as needed.

5. Cut out your paper model. Proceed with your manipulations using the card stock.

Be sure to return to your original, untwisted or flattened drawing to revise it. If you use this method, you'll have a model that you can use to cut out your metal. You will also have an original sketch that you can use again and again for future projects.

If you want to experiment with symmetrical designs, making a mirror-image model is simple and fast. You can use this approach to work out several shapes in only minutes. I use this all of the time. My drawing skills are asymmetrical at best. This helps to even things out. To make a mirror-image model, follow these steps:

1. Fold a piece of heavyweight paper in half.

2. Draw your design in pencil.

3. Cut along the lines you drew using sharp scissors.

4. Open the paper model.

Whenever you like a shape, always save your original paper. To make a duplicate model, refold the original. Place it on onto some folded paper. Trace around the edge. Cut it out, and you now have a duplicate. You can paste the duplicate directly to your metal using rubber cement in order to have a precise pattern to use as a guide for sawing the metal.

It's worth the time it takes to make a paper model. It saves your metal materials for actual projects. Plus it helps you see your designs in dimensional form. While making a model of one design, you also may discover a design you like even better.

> **ARTISAN TIP**
>
> If a paper model isn't doing the trick, try working out your design using craft wire or copper wire. Have a few different gauge sizes on hand, so you will always have some ready.

Executing Your Designs

Metalsmiths make metal objects. That's pretty straightforward. But how do they do it? They use fabrication methods. These methods include forming, forging, and shaping metal with hammers and other tools. They also include piercing and sawing metal with a jeweler's saw. They include soldering or using cold-connection methods, such as rivets, to join metal pieces. Part 2 of this book covers each of the key aspects of fabrication.

You also have to put your jewelry together in the right order. You will likely use several different techniques on jewelry you make. By thinking things through early in the game, you give your mind the critical time it needs to consider what makes most sense. For instance, you'll learn that a patina is applied as the last step in jewelry making. You won't solder jewelry after you apply a patina. But you might be able to apply texture both before and after soldering.

As a beginning metalsmith, you will be new to interpreting your ideas. Keeping them simple is helpful. You will be employing lots of time-honored techniques that have been used for hundreds of years in the creation of jewelry. But it will be your hand on the hammer, your pliers twisting the wire. There is plenty of room for your unique voice in the process. Over time, your skills will improve, and your work will come ever closer to saying exactly what you intend.

In the meantime, there are a few key things to think about as you consider creating your own jewelry designs. You will want some kind of sketch, as discussed in the previous section. It does not have to be a perfect rendering. It's for you to use as a tool.

> **ARTISAN TIP**
>
> Give your design the squint test. Close your eyes and squint at your drawing. This eliminates some detail. You'll instead get an overall view of the balance of the piece. You will see the major elements. Do they still please you? Make adjustments as needed. Even moving something 1 millimeter matters in jewelry design.

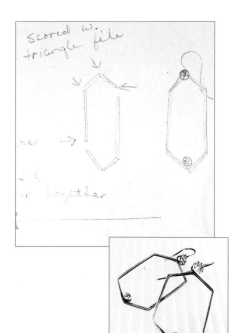

The top photo shows the design sketch with fabrication notes. The bottom photo shows the completed earrings.

As you draw up your design, ask yourself these questions:

- Does this design please me?

- How is this piece worn? Are my connections strong enough to withstand wear?

- Which type and what thickness of metal does the design use?

- Is the metal sheet, wire, or both?

- How much metal do I need?

- What needs to be soldered? Think about soldering heavier-weight items to your main piece first. Solder more delicate things last.

- Does anything require riveting? Do I have the right size of wire or tubing to make the rivet?

- Is there texture? If so, can I add the texture before or after any soldering?

- Are any of my elements formed, bent, or domed? If so, when is the best time to do that?

- Are there gemstones? If so, what kind are they and how will they be set?

- Do I need to epoxy anything, like a pearl? Time must be allowed for the epoxy to cure.

- What kind of finish does this piece have?

- Do I add a patina finish? When is the best time to add that?

- What do I use to seal the finish on my work, if anything?

- Do I have all of the tools and supplies I need to make this item?

- Do I need to make or buy anything to do my project?

- How much time do I have to devote to this project?

Some or all of these questions will come up as you make your project. The information in the following pages will help to answer some of them. Doing some of the practice projects in this book will help, too. You'll be able to go through these projects step by step and apply what you've learned to your own work. Then, come back and revisit this list when you're ready to bring your own designs to life.

Be patient with yourself. Give yourself the time you need to learn techniques well. Avoid shortcuts or hurried jobs. Take your time to do the job right the first time.

Numerous objects can inspire jewelry designs.

CHAPTER 5

Moving Metal

In This Chapter

- Evaluating metal hardness
- Forming metal
- Creating domed metal discs
- Creasing metal
- Hammering metal
- Folding metal

My earliest revelation in working with metal was that I could easily shape and bend it to my will. Forging and foldforming opened up new ways to push the metal envelope. By shaping metal, I could give jewelry forms a sculptural quality.

Forming and shaping metal can entertain and reward you for a lifetime, even if you focus your time and talents in this one area of metalsmithing alone. And you don't have to go to extremes to get started. In fact, you can start using just your hands. You can then move on to forming metal with the basic tools and approachable techniques as described in this chapter. For example, you can form domed metal discs by using a simple dapping block.

You also find out how to score and bend metal and how to strengthen it to maintain that shape. You learn that you can forge metal without a lot of force or strength. You need only a hammer, a torch, and some metal to get spectacular results fast. The chapter ends with a quick and easy overview of foldforming, a dimensional forging technique invented by Charles Lewton-Brain.

Understanding Metal Hardness

When you are thinking through the different ways to achieve a shape in metal, your tools may leap to mind. Put those aside for a minute and think about your metal first. Think about its current degree of hardness. Is it buttery soft, half-hard, or completely stiff? How thick is your metal? Is it in sheet or wire form? All of these factors will affect how easy it is to move.

You'll need to have a basic understanding of how hard your sheet or wire is so you can use the right approach when working with it. The metal will come to you with a certain amount of springiness or hardness. The amount of hardness is graded soft or dead soft, quarter-hard, half-hard, hard, and spring hard. These designations apply to both sheet and wire.

The common grades of hardness used in basic jewelry making are as follows:

- Dead soft metal is the softest, most malleable form. Dead soft metal sheet and wire can be easily bent with your hands.

- Half-hard metal is harder than dead soft, yet it is still malleable enough for you to be able to bend it with tools or even with your hands and some force.

- Hard or full-hard is, as you might expect, stiffer than half-hard. It holds its shape well, but you can still bend it using tools.

Shaping is easier if metal is annealed to the dead soft state. However, sawing, piercing, and filing are easier to do on metal that is half- or full-hard. When forging your metal with hammers, you'll need to anneal it often so it will continue to take on the shape you want. (Chapter 3 explains how to anneal and work-harden metal.)

Bending Metal Sheets and Wire

There are two basic methods of forming metal: bending and *depressing*. Bending is the less-aggressive way to form metal. In this process, the metal keeps its original thickness. Sheets and wire are moved using hands, pliers, or *mandrels*, or they can be curved using *dapping* blocks or other shapes in wood or steel.

> **DEFINITION**
>
> **Depressing** metal is forcing metal into a shaped contour, usually with the help of another shaped tool. A **mandrel** is a form around which metal may be shaped. **Dapping** is forming metal into domed circular shapes through the use of a dapping block, which is a block of wood or steel containing circular concavities used to form metal.

Discovering a World of Shaping Tools for Metal

Trusting your hands as your first metal-shaping tools is liberating. I can almost always get a shape started with my own two hands quickly and easily, and you can, too. Sometimes I employ the surface in front of me to help me ease a shape. By not imposing a tool upon the surface of metal, you can avoid denting, scratching, or scraping it. That can save on the time you spend filing and finishing. I hope you'll develop that same trust in your hands.

Sometimes, of course, you will need to use more than just your own two hands. Pliers are a key bending tool. Look for smooth jaws when purchasing pliers for jewelry making. Smooth jaws prevent your work from becoming marred. If you have serrated jaw pliers, you'll want to smooth them or cover them with electrical tape before using them on metal. Hold your pliers lightly when bending and forming metal. Instead of twisting the hand that grips the pliers, grip the metal in your free hand, and bend it around the jaws of your pliers.

> **ARTISAN TIP**
>
> You can remove the serrated texture from steel pliers by filing the jaws with an old file. Finish smoothing them with wet/dry sandpapers, used dry. Start with 220-grit, then 320-grit, and finish with 400-grit sandpaper.

Use your fingers to bend metal around pliers.

Mandrels also are important tools in jewelry making. Mandrels are metal, wood, or plastic rods or forms around which metal may be shaped. Plenty of these are available for purchase. But you can employ anything as a mandrel if it is strong enough to give you the shape you need. The great metalsmith, instructor, and author John Cogswell once told me that "The world is my mandrel." My take on this comment is to look for imaginative tool possibilities using materials available all around us.

In addition to proper ring, bracelet, and necklace mandrels, there are many other key shaping tools for metal. They include wood dowel rods and PVC pipes in various diameters cut to usable lengths, baseball bats cut to length, wood rulers, tin cans, food jars, ink pens, the side of a tabletop, steel or brass hammers, steel bench blocks, anvils of any size, and metalsmith stakes.

A dowel rod makes a handy mandrel.

Dapping Metal

Dapping metal creates domed hemisphere shapes in discs or in larger sheets of metal. Dapping blocks made of wood or metal are used to form these shapes. Each version is available with a variety of depression depths and sizes. They usually are sold in sets that contain corresponding dapping punches that fit inside the depressions. You can use discs in the depressions to make a dome. You can solder two domes to make a bead. Or you can place larger sheets of metal over the depressions to form them.

When forming metal with a dapping block, remember these two things:

1. Your metal needs to be soft.

2. Your metal, and the tool, work best when treated gently. Don't force them!

Use annealed metal or really thin metal (24 gauge or thinner) in the depressions. When your metal is in place, one good whack isn't the best way to go. It will wrinkle your metal and possibly damage the block. Your dapping tools are meant to be used in a more gentle way. Work your metal a little at a time to get a smooth, well-formed result.

If you are using a metal dapping block to dome textured metal, place a piece of paper toweling between the disc and the dapping block.

To form a domed disc, you'll need a wooden or steel dapping block and matching punches, a mallet, and some annealed metal discs. You can dome discs that are 24 gauge or thinner without annealing, if you take it slow.

To make a domed disc, follow these steps:

1. Place a disc in a dapping block depression that is larger than the disc.

2. Place a matching dapping punch in the depression over the disc, and tap it with a mallet two or three times.

3. Move the metal a little bit with the dapping punch, so it slides around in the depression. Repeat the punch/mallet tapping until the disc is evenly formed all the way around.

To get a deeper dome to your disc, you'll need to work your way down into smaller and smaller depressions, annealing your metal in between each depression size.

Scoring Metal

Metal can be shaped and formed into gentle bends in lots of ways, but sometimes you may want a sharp bend or crease in your metal sheet or wire. *Scoring* can help you create that. The process of scoring removes a lot of metal from a compact area, which is often reinforced with solder.

> **DEFINITION**
>
> **Scoring** is the removal of metal in order to create a crease or fold.

To score your metal, you'll need to cut down into it pretty deeply. You can use a sharp file or the cutoff wheel of a flexible shaft machine to do this. You may be able to score thin metal, 24 gauge or thinner, using a sharp scribe or the point of a burnishing tool. Straight lines and gentle arcs are easier to do than tightly curved lines.

To make a sharp crease in a sheet of metal, do the following:

1. Draw your fold line directly on the metal using a fine-point permanent marker.

2. Cut into the surface using a file or flexible shaft machine with cutoff wheel attachment. Wear safety goggles when using the flexible shaft machine. Touch the slowly spinning wheel to the surface of the metal and draw it forward on the metal, using small, even strokes.

3. Flip the metal over from time to time to check your progress. When you see a bulge coming through from the other side, your metal is ready to be bent.

4. Grasp the metal on either side of the fold. Using your thumbs as a fulcrum, push in on either side of the crease at the same time.

5. Clean the inside area of the crease using 400-grit wet/dry sandpaper or some Dawn dishwashing detergent, water, and a brass brush.

6. Flux along the inside of the fold line by adding hard solder at the seam. Wire solder works well for this. Heat the metal on the outside of the fold instead of the inside. Draw the heat along the seam so the solder flows the entire length of the fold.

7. Air-cool the metal, and then pickle, rinse, and dry it.

To make a sharp crease in wire, you can use a file and follow these same steps. For thinner wire, you can use a nail or a screwdriver that's been sharpened to a chisel point. This tool is handy for getting a good crease started in a prong setting.

Forging Metal

Forging is a classic metalsmithing technique. It compresses and moves the surface of the metal through the use of hammers. Forging is different from forming, because steel is used underneath metal as it's worked. This allows you to stretch and thin the metal, creating dramatic surface and edge textures that forming alone can't do.

Surfaces beneath the metal can be steel or iron anvils, polished steel blocks, or a length of old railroad tie that's been polished. Old or new, blacksmithing and silversmithing anvils are beautiful, helpful, and pricey. The good news is you don't need to buy one to do the techniques in this book. For more lightweight jobs, a steel bench block on your stable work surface will do fine.

The best heavy-duty forging setup will include a stable work surface. A solid wood work surface of at least 1½ inches (about 4 centimeters) thick or a tree stump will absorb the excess energy of hammer blows, protecting your body and making your hammering more effective. A good working height is one that allows your elbow to bend at a 90-degree angle when you're hammering. You can hammer seated or standing, the same rule of thumb applies. The following sections provide more details about tools and techniques for forging metal.

ARTISAN TIP

I own several forging hammers, but often reach for the biggest of the bunch, a 1,000-gram (2.2-pound), polished, cross-peen hammer with one wedge-shaped face and one slightly domed face. The handle has been shortened by 4 inches (about 10 centimeters) to make it easier to maneuver. It enchants me with its ability to create a delicate, lined hammer texture in no time flat.

The Importance of Every Hammer Blow

I always enjoy telling my students that "every hammer blow matters." It helps to frame your mindset if you know that hammering is a controlled operation.

Controlling the blows of your hammer is important for these four reasons:

To control work hardening. Each time your hammer lands on your metal, the metal becomes compressed. As the metal compresses, it becomes work-hardened. Anneal your metal when the movement you're able to get begins to slow down.

To control shape. Proper hammer blows easily shape your metal in the way you want it to go. Make sure your blows are headed in the right direction, have proper support underneath them, and are heavy enough to move metal.

To protect your body. Flinging your hammer down on the anvil with arms akimbo might be fun for a minute, but you'll pay the price later. Make sure you are standing or sitting in a comfortable posture. Grip the hammer with your fingers wrapped around the bottom and thumb on top like you're shaking hands with your hammer. No pointy fingers along the hammer handle. And always use the sturdiest surface you can find. Or have your chiropractor's phone number on speed dial.

To protect your tools. A smooth, clean hammer face makes all the difference in how your work looks. It leaves behind a sparkling finish and no additional cleanup work for you. Be sure to treat all of your steel tools with tender loving care. Keep them clean, dust-free, and away from moisture.

Basic Hammer Shapes

In Chapter 2, I recommend a few hammers to start you off in metalsmithing. Of these, the forging and planishing hammers are used in forging metal. These are the hammers I focus on in this section.

The planishing hammer is available in two versions and varying sizes/weights. One version has two different faces, each one slightly domed. The other has one slightly domed face and one ball face. You can use the slightly curved face to smooth the surface of metal when you want to remove hammer marks. When you want your hammer marks to take center stage, use the ball end. I always keep a highly polished planishing hammer and steel bench block or anvil on hand to create hammer textures or to work-harden ear wires and other small items.

> **DEFINITION**
>
> **Planishing** is pounding the surface of metal with a polished hammer to smooth it.

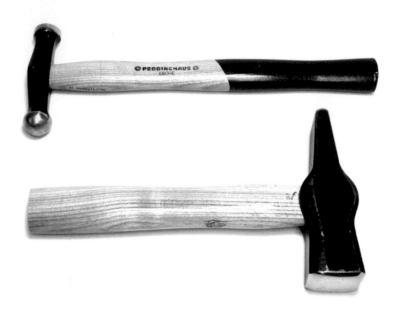

The top hammer is a planishing hammer; the bottom hammer is a forging hammer.

Forging hammers come in lots of sizes/weights. The head has one or two wedge-shaped chiseled ends that leave horizontal indentations in metal. The force of the blow pushes the metal in opposite directions, in front of and behind the hammer face. Each face is slightly different, with one end usually being more rounded than the other. In the case of a cross-peen hammer, which is also used for forging, one end is wedge-shaped, and the other is domed.

A rawhide mallet is valuable as a gentler means of moving metal and is used often in forging practices. Wooden or nylon mallets are fine substitutes. But I would avoid using rubber mallets for this purpose because the bounce factor is unpredictable and can result in pinched fingers.

The ball-peen hammer is mainly used for utility work. You can use it on small forging projects if that's what you have. You can polish the face with a progression of wet/dry sandpapers, used dry.

Fundamental Hammering Techniques

Once you understand how metal moves, it's easy to see how the face of a hammer transfers its shape to the surface of metal. To try this for yourself, grab some scrap metal and practice your hammering technique, using both wood and steel substrates. Line up all of the hammers you want to try out. Each one will give you different results.

Use sheets of metal that are around 6 inches long by 2 inches wide (15.24 centimeters long and 5.08 centimeters wide) or wire that is the same length. The thicker the wire, the better. I recommend copper for these experiments. You will get a feel for how metal moves and changes with each hammer blow. Anneal your metal to a dull red glow, quench it, and dry it before beginning. (See Chapter 3 for more on annealing metal.) You don't need to pickle your metal.

For forming metal, try using the ball end of a hammer and this practice scenario:

1. Place your annealed metal on a wood surface. The surface can have a depression or cavity.

2. Begin hammering where you want the metal to be depressed. Travel your hammer in a path of overlapping blows in a circular pattern. One full round of hammering this way is called a course.

3. Continue with the next course of hammering, around and slightly overlapping the first course. Continue with courses of hammering until the metal feels stiff, and you can no longer feel much movement beneath your hammer.

4. Anneal the metal again.

5. Continue hammering until you have achieved the shape or pattern you're after.

This earring is being forged with the ball end of a planishing hammer on a steel bench block.

Use a rawhide mallet to flatten metal.

You can use this same practice scenario with a different hammer and get different results.

To practice planishing metal to remove hammer marks, anneal the piece you used to practice forming metal, and do the following:

1. Place the annealed metal on a steel surface, such as a steel bench block.

2. Hit the metal with the flat end of a planishing hammer. Make sure the metal is in contact with the steel as you hit the metal, but avoid hitting bare steel with your hammer.

3. Continue hitting the metal in a straight line, using slightly overlapping blows, feeding your metal under the hammer. The hammer marks you made in the previous exercise will begin to smooth, and the metal will curl up on the ends. Leave some of the metal alone so you can compare the two textures and feel the difference in the flexibility of the metal.

For forging metal, try using a forging hammer and some heavy copper wire for this practice scenario:

1. Place your annealed copper wire on a steel surface, such as a bench block.

2. Hold onto one end of the copper wire, and begin hammering the metal 3 inches (7.62 centimeters) from the end of the wire. Pull the wire slowly toward you as you land the hammer blows, one blow right next to the last.

3. Watch how the metal moves when you tilt your wrist slightly to the left, then slightly to the right. The metal will make an arc when the hammer blows aren't level. Try to straighten out the wire with your hammer blows.

4. Anneal the metal and dry it well. Turn the wire over and repeat the exercise on the other three sides, creating a square wire.

You can learn a lot about what metal does from these experiments.

Foldforming

Foldforming allows you to create dimensional forms using thin sheets of metal, forging hammers, and torch heat. The technique was invented by Charles Lewton-Brain, who states, "… foldforming works at the boundaries of the natural limits of the material, where nature's rules begin to show." Lewton-Brain has written a fantastic book to explain it, appropriately called *Foldforming*.

This copper cuff bracelet is the result of both forging and foldforming.

(© Paul D'Andrea)

Foldforming allows the plastic qualities of metal to shine. You can't help but notice the organic qualities that are revealed in the completed forms. Although you can solder or use rivets on completed forms, there are many designs where that's not necessary.

In order to do foldforming, you'll need these basic tools and supplies:

- Torch setup or kiln for a large, hot flame to easily and quickly anneal your metal. A high-heat torch, such as the acetylene/ambient air plumber's torch, works well.

- Running water or a quart-size or larger container of water for quenching.

- Copper tongs.

- Metal shears.

- A dull knife, screwdriver, or toothbrush with the head cut off at an angle to pry open the forms.

- Forging hammer with V-shaped ends or slightly rounded V-shaped ends or a cross-peen forging hammer with one V-shaped and one slightly domed end.

- Rawhide mallet.

- Steel supporting surface, such as a bench block, anvil, or a length of railroad tie.

- A 3 × 6-inch (7.62 × 15.24-centimeter) or larger sheet of 24-gauge or 16-ounce copper, such as roofing copper (.5 millimeter thick).

Foldforms typically start with a sheet of annealed metal and involve five steps:

1. Fold the sheet and tighten the fold by bringing the edges together using your fingers and then using the mallet to pound the fold closed. Or hold a portion of the metal at an angle and place it just off the edge of an anvil or bench block. Strike along the angle to form a crease.

2. Forge the folded sheet by using the V-shaped face of your hammer to hit along the seam, without hitting the supporting steel below. This takes some practice! Slightly overlap your hammer blows. Start at one end of the metal and travel to the other. Do two courses of hammering.

Hammer the seam of the folded copper sheet to forge it.

3. Anneal the metal. Allow metal to heat to a bright orange glow and quench it immediately in the water. Dry it well before proceeding. You can continue to hammer, or you can unfold the sheet.

The photograph on the left shows copper being annealed to a bright orange. The photograph on the right shows copper being quenched after annealing.

4. Unfold the sheet. Use a dull knife, screwdriver, or a toothbrush with the head cut off at an angle to pry the metal apart. Then use your fingers to open the fold.

Open the folded copper form using a headless toothbrush.

5. Pound the metal with a mallet to open the fold completely. Optionally, you can use the forging hammer, with a steel surface underneath, to "confirm" the fold. Use the hammer on the seam, slightly overlapping the blows. You can also refold the metal either before or after you confirm the fold.

Confirm the fold with a forging hammer.

Sawing and Piercing Metal

In This Chapter

- Jeweler's saw questions and answers
- Steps for loading a saw blade
- Two low-tech, easy ways to make holes in metal
- Instructions for using handheld and motorized drills

The techniques of sawing and piercing go hand in hand. Although the methods are simple, you may have lots of questions. I have lots of tips and tricks to offer about these techniques, too.

This chapter starts with several questions and answers regarding the key tool for sawing on metal: the jeweler's saw. I also include step-by-step instructions on how to use this tool. And I get into whether you need lubricant for your saw blade. (Hint: You don't. Read on to find out why.)

At some point, you are going to want to pierce holes in your metal. This chapter fills you in on low-tech and higher-tech ways to do this. Before you use a drill to make holes, however, I recommend that you read all the way through the last section of this chapter. It provides helpful information about drill bits and steps for using both handheld and motorized drills.

Working with a Jeweler's Saw

The jeweler's saw has been around for hundreds of years. This thin saw blade under tension in a saw frame can cut both ferrous and nonferrous metals and is one of the first tools that many metalsmiths learn to use. It has a straightforward design in an open C shape with a handle on the bottom and three screws. Two thumb screws on the front of the frame allow the user to change blades, and a single set screw on the far side of the C-shaped frame allows the user to adjust the height of the saw frame up and down, depending on the length of the blade.

A jeweler's saw can be used for more than cutting a shape out of flat metal or tubing. It also can be used to cut wood, paper, laminates, plastics, waxes (with a spiral blade), and even steel. Multiple shapes taped or glued together can be cut out at once with some accuracy. The saw also can be used as a miniature file in tight places. Jewelry of incredible beauty, depth, and detail can be created using this one simple tool.

I encourage you to take some time to get to know the jeweler's saw. Read through all of the information in these pages. Draw random designs using a permanent marker on scrap metal. Include sharp angles and gentle curved lines. Use these to make test cuts, following lines as best you can. Don't worry if blades break. Each broken blade is a badge of honor that moves you one step closer to masterful sawing.

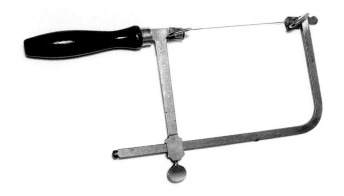

The jeweler's saw is a central component in metalsmithing.

How to Handle a Jeweler's Saw

Using a flimsy-looking jeweler's saw and miniscule saw blade to cut metal is not entirely intuitive. How well this talent is learned is often related to how kindly it is later perceived. Taking time to learn how to mount a saw blade under tension and how to use a saw frame properly really pays off.

A death grip on the handle will kill the joy of the jeweler's saw and break lots of blades. Easy does it is the key. You want to develop friendly terms with your saw, so remember to keep it loose. Some jewelers float in a Zen-like state while sawing. It can be a lovely experience. However, if your project can be cut out with aviation shears, by all means use them!

You probably have some questions about the jeweler's saw. Read the following answers to get more information about the saw frame and blade:

What if I'm left-handed? Thumb screws on jeweler's saws are typically mounted to accommodate right-handed people, but the nuts and screws can be removed and switched to the other side of the frame for lefties.

What size frame should I buy? Frames may be purchased in a 3- or 4-inch (about 8- or 10-centimeter) depth to accommodate moving the blade around a piece of sheet metal. Deeper frames are available for working with larger pieces of metal. Think about what you want to make and get a saw frame that will accommodate it. Keep in mind that shorter frames are easier to handle.

How do I hold the saw frame? Saw frames are used in a vertical position with a straight up-and-down motion like that of a sewing machine. It's important to keep the saw moving in a gentle up-and-down motion.

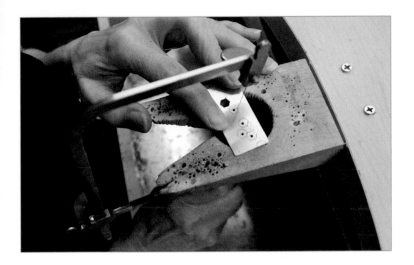

Use a jeweler's saw with an up-and-down motion to cut shapes within metal.

What is a jeweler's saw blade? A jeweler's saw blade is a thin strip of hardened steel with uniformly spaced and angled teeth that is used under tension in a jeweler's saw frame to cut metal.

What size blade should I buy? Saw blades come in 16 sizes, from 8/0 (smallest) to 8 (largest). The general guideline is 3 teeth per width of metal. The teeth are angled outward in rows called sets. Having three teeth against the width of your metal keeps the blade traveling true as the sets remove little chips.

How do I use this bundle of blades I just bought? Saw blades are sold by the dozen. They arrive wrapped in a very fine wire that needs to be gently unraveled before a blade can be teased out of its nest. It is easier to do this if you tease the blade out with the teeth pointing away rather than toward you. This direction helps keep the blades from catching on each other as well. Saw blades are loaded under tension with the frame in a horizontal position. See "How to Load a Saw Blade" for that information.

Saw blades are small, but they can do a lot.

> **ARTISAN TIP**
>
> I do most work at the bench with 3/0, 2/0 and 1/0 blades. You don't need to own every single blade size available. Match the thickness of metal to the size blade you need by allowing for three teeth per thickness of metal. Over time, you will choose your own favorite blade sizes to work with.

What is a spiral saw blade used for? Spiral-shaped blades are used for plastic, wax, and acrylic items. Saw blades heat up during use. Plastics and waxes will melt around a standard straight blade, bind up, and break the blade quicker than spit. Spiral blades prevent that from happening. They are available from the same suppliers that provide straight jeweler's saw blades.

How to Load a Saw Blade

To load a saw blade into a jeweler's saw frame, follow these steps:

1. Select the proper blade. The rule of thumb is three teeth per thickness of metal.

2. Loosen the thumb screws. These are the two screws located at the top and bottom of the frame. Loosen them just enough to accommodate the thin saw blade.

3. Support the frame for loading. Seated at your bench with about a foot (.3 meters) of space between you and your bench, hold the frame horizontally in your dominant hand. Nestle the handle against your shoulder or breastbone and the top of the frame against the bench. The open C shape should point toward the ceiling. If you were to let your hands go, the frame would not drop to the floor. Now the frame is well-supported.

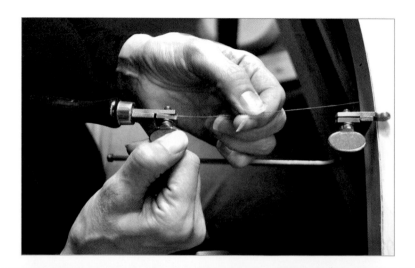

Support the saw frame with your body while you load the saw blade.

4. Get the blade. Make sure the teeth are pointed downwards, towards your chest. It's often easier to feel this than to see it. Gently stroke your finger along the edge of the blade, checking for the teeth to catch.

5. With the blade teeth pointed towards your chest, lay the blade into the opening between the frame and the thumb screw's small washer or compression plate.

6. Tighten one screw.

7. Important! Lay the blade into the other opening. Move forward slightly to make the frame bow inward a bit. Tighten the screw, keeping the pressure on. This key step helps create the tension needed to saw your metal.

8. Release pressure on the frame to create tension in the blade.

9. Take the edge of your finger and tweak the blade like you would pluck a violin string, listening for the "Ping!" If the blade is not tight enough, the sound will be low and dull. If this is the case, repeat steps 5 through 8 until you get a ping sound.

Lean in when you tighten the second screw on the saw frame.

How to Use Bench Pin When Sawing

When you are sawing, a bench pin clamped to a stable surface is an essential friend and sawing facilitator. It is important to use either a bench pin or a small piece of board secured to your work surface to support metal as it is being cut. Most jeweler's benches come with a slot in front to accommodate a bench pin, and some benches create a uniform surface from pin to table top, furthering the area available for supported sawing operations. If you don't have such a bench, a C-clamp can hold a bench pin to any solid surface, giving you an instant work surface. Place the clamp on your nondominant side.

Make any modifications you want to trick out your bench pin to suit you and your work style. Cutting a V shape in a plain piece of wood will help provide support. Divots cut or drilled into the surface or side of the pin offer other ways to stabilize metal, wire, or tubing by creating nooks and crannies for these things so they can be more easily held and cut. A hole drilled part of the way through the top of the bench pin will secure tiny things like earring posts. See Chapter 1 for more information about bench pins.

A bench pin provides support for your metal and space to maneuver the jeweler's saw.

Why Saw Blade Lubricants Are Optional

In most corners of the jewelry-making world, conventional wisdom dictates that jeweler's saw blades require lubricant. Blade lubricants such as Bur-Life and beeswax have been in use for years. Spit even has been employed in getting a stubborn saw blade to unstick. When I started out in metalsmithing years ago, I was a devoted user of saw blade lubricants. Then an unconventional wisdom was revealed to me via Thomas Mann's book *Metal Artist's Workbench: Demystifying the Jeweler's Saw.* I first wanted the book solely due to a high regard for Mr. Mann and his work and because he offered signed copies. I did not feel I needed help with sawing, though.

Once the book arrived, I began reading the information Mann collected and condensed through 40 years of firsthand experience at the jeweler's bench. I paid attention. Very soon, I gave up blade lubricant and have not felt the need to go back. The visual mess and clutter of the lubricant gone, I can see the metal better. I can see the lines to follow better. I even feel the metal better. If there is a Zen to using the jeweler's saw, I was able to find the way there more easily without the lubricant than with it.

Saw blade lubricant is a personal preference on the part of many metalsmiths. I may be in the minority. For me, the answer is no lubricant on my blade. If you feel you must use lube, apply it only to the back of the blade, rather than the teeth. The back of the blade is the area that binds. Applying lubricant to the teeth will clog them.

Using Low-Tech Piercing Methods

Ever wonder how intricate designs are cut into the middle of a piece of metal? It's easy once you know how. Plus, there are lots of ways to do it.

Piercing goes hand in hand with using a jeweler's saw. You may require a simple hole to thread an ear wire for earrings. Or you may have a design that requires your saw blade to travel within the border of your metal. Certain designs are centered on a series of pierced holes of different sizes. In any of these situations, you need a way to pierce some type of hole in the middle of your metal. In this section, I tell you about several ways to accomplish this task.

The Simplest Hole Punch

With a common nail and a ball-peen hammer, you can quickly pierce a hole in most soft metals. The metal must be thin enough to have the entire nail point go through. Generally, a nail goes through up to about 18-gauge metal, but you may need to experiment. This method works best on a hard wood surface.

To make a hole in metal using a nail, follow these steps:

1. Place your metal on the wood surface.

2. Place your nail on the metal, wherever your hole is needed.

3. Strike the head of your nail with the flat face of the ball-peen hammer.

4. Check to see whether the nail has gone through your metal. Repeat step 3 until you have a hole that is the correct size.

The drawback to this method is that it creates a rough hole with an outward dimple. That might be just fine for your project. If it isn't fine, use a half-round metal file on the protruding edges of the hole to file them smooth. Stick a round, pointed burnisher into the hole and twirl it around to slightly widen the hole and smooth the inside rim. Finish with sandpaper if needed.

Hole-Punching Pliers

Several types of pliers on the market enable you to easily punch holes into metal with your own two hands. The most reasonably priced pliers will punch small holes in 24-gauge metal. That's fairly thin metal. Pliers that punch larger holes or holes in thicker metal are priced higher. Look for pliers made with high-carbon steel, which provides the strength needed to punch round holes in thick metal without becoming damaged. You can also find pliers that punch oval and square-shaped holes. Think of the design possibilities with those!

Hole-punching pliers make it easy to pierce metal.

METAL MISHAP

Sometimes hole-punching pliers create small marks on the metal. For this reason, you should test them first on scrap metal. When you know how your pliers mark metal, you can plan your design accordingly.

Drilling

If you have access to a hand drill, a spiral hand drill, a drill press, or a flexible shaft machine, you'll have even more ways to easily make holes in metal. You will need drill bits in assorted sizes. Twist drill bits are used in wood and metal to create holes. Look for bits labeled HS or HSS (high-speed steel). When working with any drill bit, you must use a lubricant often. Be sure to read the specific information later in the chapter for more information on drill bits. Refer to the Appendix B for a drill bit guide that includes sizes.

Supply List and Basic Drilling Preparation Steps

You will need the following basic supplies for all drilling techniques:

Drill bits in appropriate sizes

Lubricant for drill bits, like beeswax or Bur-Life

Small steel block

Scrap piece of wood

Center punch or nail

Hammer

Goggles

Half-round file

Wet/dry sandpaper, 320 grit

You will need to use a *chuck key* when inserting or removing the drill bit in a flexible shaft machine. Some drill presses need a chuck key, while others are equipped with a keyless chuck. That means you can tighten the chuck by hand. You won't need a chuck key for the handheld drill or the spiral hand drill. They have keyless chucks.

I'm using a chuck key to tighten a bristled polishing bur as I place it in a handpiece for my flexible shaft machine.

> **DEFINITION**
>
> A **chuck key** is a small device used to tighten or loosen the chuck opening of a drill. The gears on a chuck key match the gears on the chuck. Chuck keys come in various sizes to match the corresponding chucks.

Most drilling processes follow these basic steps:

1. Place your metal on the steel surface.

2. Tap the head of a nail or center punch with a hammer to make a small dent in the metal where you want the hole.

3. Replace the steel surface with a piece of wood.

4. Insert your drill bit into the chuck, and tighten it by hand or with a chuck key.

5. Lubricate the bit. Use your choice of lubricants.

Your drill bit is now ready to use. Read the following sections for the specific ways to complete your drilled hole using a handheld or motorized drill.

Use a center punch to make a dent in your metal before drilling a hole.

Hand Drills and Spiral Hand Drills

If you have a hand drill or a spiral hand drill for making holes in metal, it's pretty simple to do. Both feature a keyless chuck. That means you can tighten and loosen the chuck by hand, without additional tools.

To use a hand drill, get the basic supplies from the supply list above. Then follow the previous steps 1 through 5 for basic drilling processes. Once you have your drill bit in place and it is lubricated, proceed with the following steps:

1. With the drill perfectly vertical, place the point of the bit in the dent you have already made.

2. Hold the handle at the top of the drill in your nondominant hand and hold the turning handle in your dominant hand. Slowly turn the turning handle. If your metal spins, you will need to clamp it down with a C-clamp.

3. Periodically stop drilling to clear the metal shavings away from the drill bit. Once you have gone through the metal, you might see wood shavings from the scrap of wood under your metal. That's your cue to stop drilling.

I am using a hand drill to make a hole in a piece of metal.

ARTISAN TIP

You can use the hand drill to make decorative twisted wire. Use annealed square wire, any gauge. Keep the length to 3 feet (91 centimeters) or less. One end of the annealed wire goes in the hand drill. The other end goes in a vise. Then pull on the hand drill to create tension and keep the wire straight and gently twist. Don't twist too much or the wire will kink. This process also work-hardens wire, so you may want to anneal it again. This decorative twisted wire makes distinctive jump rings.

Clear any shavings of metal from the hole you made. If your hole is rough, use a half-round metal file to smooth it. Or you can use 320-grit wet/dry sandpaper, dry, to smooth it.

The spiral hand drill is a much smaller tool. It is about the size of an ink pen and has a twisted design. Its small size means that it can pierce thin metal only.

To use the spiral hand drill, you need the same basic supplies mentioned in the beginning of the drilling section. Then insert your drill bit in the adjustable chuck. With one finger resting on the top of the drill, push the knurled plunger up and down. This action creates the spin that will cause the bit to move into the small dent in your metal. Continue to work the spiral hand drill until you have a hole. Perform any cleanup needed to the edges of the hole with some wet/dry sandpaper, used dry.

Motorized Drills

Using power tools is the next step up in drilling holes in your metal. It's fast and easy. I recommend using a small drill press (tabletop size) or a flexible shaft machine to do this job. Either of these works well when you have a lot of holes to drill. For either machine, the drill bit should always spin as you apply it to and remove it from the metal. This keeps the bit from bogging down or catching in the metal. Applying lubricant often during the process helps, too. It also protects your expensive drill bits.

To drill holes using a drill press, you will need the basic supplies listed in the beginning of the Drilling section. Be sure to use your goggles as well. Firmly hold onto larger pieces of metal using your nondominant hand. Use a pair of pliers to hold pieces of metal smaller than 1 inch across. This keeps them from spinning away from you if the bit catches.

Follow the five steps for basic drilling preparation. Once you have your drill bit in place and it is lubricated, proceed with the following steps to complete the process:

1. Place a piece of flat scrap wood on the drill press table.

2. Place your metal on the scrap of wood.

3. Position the metal. Place the metal so the dent is directly under the drill bit. Test the position by pulling down the press handle without switching on the power. Reposition metal so the dent meets the point of the bit.

4. Grip the metal. Use your nondominant hand or a pair of pliers.

5. Turn on the drill. Use a slow speed if possible.

6. Pull down the arm gently to precisely meet the dent in the metal. Hold the metal firmly. Don't push the arm down with force—it can harm or break off the drill bit.

7. As spiral-shaped shavings of metal appear, raise the arm of the drill. Clear the shavings from the area to keep them from clogging the hole.

8. Repeat the pausing and clearing. Continue pulling down the arm, gently drilling, and lifting the arm.

9. When the drill bit pierces through the metal, you will see some wood shavings appear from the scrap of wood under your metal. When that happens, raise the arm while the bit is spinning. Then stop the drill.

You should be able to get through thin metal in only one or two pause-and-clear cycles. It will take longer with thicker metal. In fact, it could take several patient minutes of drilling and clearing. Lubricate your drill bit after every other pause-and-clear cycle to keep it clean and cool.

> **METAL MISHAP**
>
> It's tempting to pull down hard on the arm of a drill press. Don't do it! It could cause the bit to become stuck in the metal. (If the bit does get stuck, stop the drill and gently untwist the metal from the bit.) Worse, the bit could break off into your metal. If this happens, you can dissolve the bit with alum. (This is the same stuff used to make pickles.) Use a concentrated amount of alum and water and simmer your item with the broken bit in it for about 20 minutes. Use Corning Ware or Pyrex for this job. Don't use a stainless steel pan—it will succumb to the alum.

The final power tool in this chapter is the flexible shaft machine. It has a powerful motor that has a lot of torque. The motor attaches to a spinning coil in a rubbery sheath that powers a small handpiece. You control the speed of the handpiece with a foot pedal or dial. It will easily handle most metal drilling tasks you will face. It has the added benefit of variable speed. Also, a number 30 adjustable chuck handpiece will hold even the tiniest of drill bits and a wide assortment of other burs and bits.

Models range from motors with $\frac{1}{10}$ to $\frac{1}{3}$ horsepower with speeds from 500 to 18,000 RPM (revolutions per minute). A versatile choice for most metalsmiths will be a motor of at least $\frac{1}{8}$ horsepower and up to 18,000 RPM powering a number 30 handpiece controlled by a foot pedal. Many machines today also offer a switch for alternating the direction of the motor. This feature is helpful in the removal of a stuck drill bit, but it's not essential. Foredom is the industry leader in flexible shaft machines, offering many model types and price points. Low-cost, entry-level models are offered by Prodigy ($\frac{1}{8}$ horsepower, 20,000 RPM motor) and Grobet USA ($\frac{1}{10}$ horsepower, 18,000 RPM motor) for around $100.

If you have used a drill press to drill a hole into metal, the same basic principles apply when you use the flexible shaft machine. The key difference is that you guide the drill bit into the metal yourself. You also use a bench pin or a small block of wood. Gather the same basic supplies listed at the beginning of the "Drilling" section and follow the basic steps to prepare your metal for drilling by making a dent in the metal to help guide your drill bit. Don't forget to wear your safety goggles!

Follow these guidelines for drilling with the flexible shaft machine:

1. Place your metal on your bench pin or small block of wood. When I'm drilling holes in metal, I use a bench pin to support my work. I drill right down into the bench pin when I go through the metal. It doesn't bother me one bit. If it bothers you, you can use the small block of wood instead.

2. Grip the metal. Use your nondominant hand to hold the metal firmly to the surface of the bench pin.

3. Hold the handpiece as vertically as possible. Position your thumb in the indentation at the top of the handpiece as a guide. Pretend that your arm is like that of a drill press. It moves slowly up and down, never wandering from side to side.

> **SAFE 'SMITHING**
>
> Handheld rotary tools (Dremel is a common brand) contain the motor within the handpiece. These tools don't usually have the torque that a drill bit requires to make it all the way through metal. As a result, the bit can grab and, like an out-of-control food processor, make a sharp, spinning blade out of your metal. For this reason, I do not recommend using a handheld rotary tool for piercing metal.

4. Gently push the foot pedal until the drill begins to spin. Use a slow speed. There is no need to go fast, but go fast enough that the bit moves.

5. Lower the handpiece so the drill bit precisely meets the dent in the metal. Hold the metal firmly. Don't push the drill bit with force into the metal. It can harm or break off the drill bit.

6. As spiral-shaped shavings of metal appear, raise the handpiece from the metal with the drill bit spinning. Clear the shavings to keep them from clogging the hole.

7. Repeat the pausing and clearing as needed.

8. When the drill bit pierces through the metal and you see some wood shavings appear from the scrap of wood or bench pin under your metal, remove the drill bit from the metal. Allow the motor to stop.

You probably can get through thin metal in only one or two pause-and-clear cycles. It takes longer with thicker metal. In fact, it could take several patient minutes of drilling and clearing. Lubricate your drill bit after every other pause-and-clear cycle to keep it clean and cool.

Here is how to hold a flexible shaft handpiece when you drill metal.

> **ARTISAN TIP**
>
> Listen to your flexible shaft machine. When it is in optimum use, the motor purrs. At faster speeds, it purrs louder. A motor that whines, chatters, or groans is being stressed. Listen to your motor. It will tell you if you are doing something incorrectly. Pay attention, and it will reward you with years of reliable service.

The appearance of wood shavings indicates that the drill bit on the flexible shaft handpiece has pierced the metal.

Drill Bits

Drill bits are an essential tool in all drilling techniques. Twist drill bits are used to create holes in metal. Look for bits labeled HS or HSS (high-speed steel). I rely on drill bits purchased through specialty suppliers for the jewelry maker. I've had much better luck with the sharpness and longevity of these bits. It's disappointing to buy a bargain pack of bits at the mega box do-it-all center, only to find that they have dulled after two uses.

Use a lubricant often when working with any drill bit. The high-speed spinning as the bit contacts your metal creates a lot of heat. The lubricant helps cool the bit and reduce friction. It reduces chatter and helps to prolong the life of your high-speed drill bits. Some proprietary brands are Bur Life and Bur Lube. These lubricants come in paste, liquid, or solid stick forms. You also can use beeswax as a drill bit lubricant. I keep containers of liquid and paste Bur Life next to my tabletop drill press. At the bench, I keep a stick of Bur Life jammed in the corner. That way I can dip my slowly spinning drill bit into it with one hand.

Remember that drill bits will create a hole slightly larger than the bit itself. This is an important point to remember when you need to make a hole that's a specific size, as you do, for example, when riveting. (Riveting is covered in Chapter 8.)

Appendix B has a handy guide on drill bit sizes and corresponding metal gauges and saw blade sizes.

Filing and Smoothing Metal

In This Chapter

- Selecting the right file for the job
- Using and taking care of files
- Smoothing metal with sandpaper
- Polishing metal with burnishing tools

In this chapter, you learn the ins and outs of filing and smoothing metal surfaces. Filing, sanding, and smoothing are foundational techniques in making metal jewelry. Metal files come in lots of sizes and tons of shapes, from tiny to big. They come in different cutting surfaces, even when they look pretty much the same. I help make easy work of how to tell the difference and select the right file for the right job. I also give you a list of the files I recommend when you're starting out.

You also get lots of basic information on the various ways to use sandpapers, emery papers, polishing papers, and other ways to smooth metal. I have my favorites here, and I'll tell you what they are and why I like them. You also learn about the proper progression for using sandpapers to best effect.

Polishing methods for motorized tools, such as the flexible shaft machine, are mentioned, too. Throughout, you get handy tips and tricks to help focus your efforts and give you great results.

Filing

Files for metalworking are steel hand tools used to shape, smooth, score, and texture metal. The precision cutting surfaces of files are invaluable in metalsmithing. Their proper use can make a big difference in your finished jewelry. That's why you want to look for and use proper metalsmithing files.

Basic File Facts

Most files are one unit of metal that narrows at one end. The narrow end is called the tang and is used as the grip portion of a file. Files are sold without handles. You may cover the tang with a handle, or not.

Files perform their function through the rows of teeth cut into their surface. The number of teeth in the rows determines the grade of a file. This grading system runs coarsest to finest, with 00 being the coarsest and 6 being the finest. The more cutting teeth a file has, the higher the number it is assigned. These grades are known as cuts. Note, however, that German, Swiss, and American files have different standards and cuts. These comparisons are usually spelled out when you purchase files. German-cut files start coarser than Swiss-cut files, for example, and go finer.

There are two types of toothed cutting surfaces. Single-cut files have one parallel row of ordered cutting lines and cross-cut (or double-cut) files have two rows of cutting lines crossing over one another. I prefer cross-cut files.

> **ARTISAN TIP**
>
> A wine cork makes a nice file handle. Just insert the tang into the cork and tap the cork firmly with a hammer. To quickly identify files, write the number and silhouette on the cork using a permanent marker.

Some files have a safe edge, which is a side with no cutting surface. Safe edges come in handy when you are filing in tight spaces because they prevent you from cutting into areas of your metal that you want protected.

Files come in many sizes and shapes. For best results, look for a close match between the size and shape of the file and the metal you are filing. The next section describes some of the types and shapes of files that are available.

Types and Shapes of Metal Files

There are a few different types, and a lot of different shapes, of metalworking files. Each does something slightly different from the other.

The most common file types are hand, escapement, needle, and riffler. A hand file is 8 inches long (20 centimeters). It is the longest and widest type of file, and the one I use most often.

The *escapement file* is 5½ inches (14 centimeters) long and is also known as a square-handled needle file. Escapement files split the difference between hand files and needle files. I reach for these when hand files are too big.

It's easy to see where the needle file gets its name. At 4 inches (10 centimeters) long, needle files are smaller, thinner, and meant for more delicate tasks than other types of files. I like larger files because I have large hands, but needle files still see occasional use in my studio.

A *riffler file* is 6 or 7 inches (15 or 18 centimeters) long with 1 to 1½ inches (3 to 4 centimeters) of cutting surface at one end or both shaped ends. Riffler files are not often used, but they are perfect for certain jobs where a curved file is required.

Within those types of files, you can find different cuts, which means how fine the teeth are. A finer cut will have a higher cut number assigned to it. For instance, a number 2 cut hand file will remove metal more aggressively than a number 3 cut hand file.

Specialty files are made for people involved in lapidary work (cutting of gemstones), glass work, and model building for casting purposes. These files are available in varying shapes and sizes, singly and in sets. There are three types of specialty files:

- Diamond files are used for glass, stone, and other hard surfaces.
- Wax-carving files are used to shape wax models for casting.
- Valtitan files are used for platinum and titanium work.

There is also a type of file you can use to create a unique texture on the surface of your metal. A checkering (or texturing) file is a flat file with a broad rectangular surface and deep-cut teeth on the two broad sides. This file creates a Florentine, or cross-hatch finish, on metal. It is available in various cut numbers. It's a more expensive file option than most.

That's not all you need to know about files! Besides getting an understanding of the types, you also need to know about the available shapes. The same type of file can be made in a number of different shapes.

These shapes of files are common options:

- A flat file has a broad rectangular surface, with teeth on three sides.
- A half-round file has a low dome, tapers to a point, and includes teeth on all sides.
- A half-round ring file has a higher, half-dome; tapers to a point; and includes teeth on all sides.
- A barrette file has a low profile, with teeth on broad side only. Its sides angle inward and taper to a point.
- A crossing file is a double half-round needle file that tapers to a point, with teeth on all sides.
- On a square file, the four edges taper to a point, and all sides have teeth.
- On a triangle (or three-square) file, three edges taper to a point, and all sides have teeth.

Buy the best metalworking files you can afford. In Chapter 2, I recommend starting out with at least a number 2 cut half-round hand file, a number 2 cut flat hand file, and a set of needle files for the bare minimum setup. Add the number 3 cut barrette hand file next. Continue to add to your collection with the other suggestions I've made in that same chapter. The right file will make quick, enjoyable work of all your filing tasks.

ARTISAN TIP

When deciding on files for purchase, you might need a tipping point. When all else is even, go for the bigger file if you have large hands, and go for the smaller file if you have small hands.

Filing Techniques

Now that you have selected a few files to use, you need to learn how to use them properly. First, hold the file in your dominant hand. No pointy fingers! Grasp your files as though you were turning a key in a lock. Don't use your index finger to guide the file. The pointy finger method eventually impinges on nerves, which hurts.

No filing in midair! Don't float your arms or walk about while filing. Remain seated with your feet flat on the floor. Keep your elbows pinned close to your body for stability. Also, support your work by leaning it against your work surface; pressing it against your bench pin; or holding it in a *ring clamp*, pliers with jaws covered by electrical tape, or vice grips.

To file your metal, apply pressure on the forward stroke. Then lift the file lightly to draw it back towards you. Keep in mind that files cut only on the forward stroke and only in one direction. Using a harsh back-and-forth sawing motion will dull teeth. Also, filing too much is a common mistake in the beginning. Just a few strokes of the file can be enough to do the job. Laying the file sideways across work creates a gentler cutting action, known as cross-filing, and may be the right approach in certain situations.

> **DEFINITION**
>
> A **ring clamp** has two working ends with a hinge in the middle and a tapered wedge. Rings and other small pieces of metal are placed in one side of the clamp. The wedge is pushed firmly in the other side to grip work. Typically this tool is made from wood, but it also is available in metal or plastic versions.

A bench pin provides support for this filing job.

The cross-filing technique works for this round disc.

Depending on the shape of metal you are handling, you should use different filing techniques. For example, to file flat metal easily, lay the file down on your work surface. Hold your metal in your dominant hand, and pin the file to your work surface with your other hand. Run the metal across the file's surface until it's as smooth as needed. If your file has a handle, make sure it extends over the edge of your workbench in order to maintain a level filing surface.

Use this filing technique when working with flat metal.

To file inside curves, use a round, half-round or half-round ring file with a rolling motion, pushing forward as you go. Pull the file up slightly on the backward stroke. This way you can smoothly remove metal all around the curved surface without creating flat spots.

You can enlarge or smooth holes with a round or a half-round file. Count your strokes as you move the file around the hole to keep things perfectly even. You can use a *broach*, reamer, or burnishing tool to enlarge holes, too. Use a broach or reamer to file around the perimeter of the hole evenly and gently. Or insert a burnishing tool in the hole and turn it a few times to widen the hole a bit.

Filing a round hole takes a gentle touch.

When enlarging holes, be patient. Never twist or jam the file down into the hole, or try to stretch the metal by using the file as a lever. The tip of your file could become stuck or even break off.

Lastly, make sure to tap files on your work surface to clear shavings whenever you file. This action dislodges tiny metal bits and keeps files in good cutting shape.

> **DEFINITION**
>
> A **broach** is a small, slender, five-sided, very sharp cutting tool that is used to enlarge holes, particularly when a specific opening size is needed. Broaches work by shaving minute particles of metal from the circumference of a hole. These tiny tools come in packages containing a range of different sizes. Handles are attached, or a pin vise can be used to hold smaller broach sizes. Broaches are sharp, flexible, precise instruments. Use care when working with them. They look dainty but slice well, no matter what the surface, including your skin. A set of broaches can cost anywhere from $12 to $35.

Special Care for Your Files

Metalworking files are precision instruments and are priced accordingly. Experience has taught me that it is worth it to invest in good-quality hand files. I grab mine every day, and they need to be reliable. Once you invest in metalworking files, you need to make sure that you protect these important assets.

Files that rub together can quickly dull their valuable cutting edges. Store files in such as way as they are separated from one another. Here are three great ideas for file storage:

Organize with plastic pipe. Measure files, subtracting the length of the file handle. Use this measurement to cut lengths of 1-inch plastic PVC pipe. Store these upright within easy reach of your bench, or attach PVC caps to the bottom and attach these pipes to the bench leg nearest your dominant hand.

Organize with pockets. Purchase a premade canvas tool organizer to hang on or near your bench. Or, if you sew, buy a couple of yards of heavy canvas or oilcloth and sew pockets to accommodate your file sizes. Add grommets for handy hanging near your bench. When traveling, you can easily take your files with you in this organizer, and they'll stay protected.

Organize with magnetism. Hang a magnetic strip near your bench and place your files on it. This method works as long as you do your work in a climate-controlled area where rust is not a concern.

If your studio is not climate controlled, or you live in a damp or humid environment, you need to protect files and all steel tools from rust by storing them carefully. One way to do this is to place moisture-absorbent packets rescued from the purchase of goods that contain them, such as shoes, handbags, or electronics, in closed drawers or containers along with files. Alternately, you can purchase rechargeable tins containing moisture-absorbent pellets. These can be dried out in a home oven and reused repeatedly. Place them in the drawers or containers along

> **METAL MISHAP**
>
> Don't coat files with heavy oil. It clogs the fine cutting surfaces.

with your files. A light coat of WD-40 also will displace water and protect the surface of your files from future rust. It won't remove rust, though.

One last filing tip: don't rely on steel file cards to clean out files, as tiny bits of steel may break off into the cuts of the file, doing more harm than good. Instead, clear files by occasionally tapping them on the edge of your bench as you work.

Sanding

After filing, sanding is the next step in smoothing metal, and it's an important skill that you'll use often on your metalworking projects. Sanding is used to refine the rough spots in metal. It removes file marks, surface blemishes, and small amounts of errant solder. It prepares your metal for polishing, or it can be used as a final polish all on its own. (Chapter 13 has more information about polishing your jewelry.)

You can sand metal by hand or with power. I focus on hand sanding techniques in this section. However, you can use a flexible shaft machine or a Dremel tool fitted with a flap wheel attachment, a split mandrel that holds a strip of sandpaper, or a sanding disc that fits into a mandrel using a screw.

You can do a lot with sandpapers and sanding materials, and there are lots from which you can choose. I make it easier in this section by narrowing down the options. I also explain how to make your own sanding sticks for pennies. Finally, you will learn that sometimes you only need one type of sandpaper to get the results you need. Other times, you need to use a sanding progression to get the job done.

Select the Right Sandpapers and Abrasives

Sandpapers are known by many names, such as abrasive paper, emery paper, polishing paper, and glass paper. Each uses different cutting media, either natural or man-made grit, adhered to a backing material. All sandpapers are graded using a numbering system. The higher the number is, the finer the grit.

Some sandpapers are labeled as wet/dry sandpaper and can be used with water. I recommend you use wet/dry sandpapers when working with metal. They hold up longer than regular sandpapers. Wet/dry sandpapers are available at automotive stores and hardware stores. 3M makes a tough wet/dry sandpaper called Tri-Mite.

For sandpaper, I prefer to use wet/dry silicon carbide in 220, 320, and 400 grits for most hand-sanding activities. You could use 500-grit sandpaper for a finer, glossier finish, but I rarely feel the need for it. Silicon carbide sandpapers are black in color. Emery papers are similar and are used mostly for finishing. They are dark gray in color. Both will work well on metal.

ARTISAN TIP

Sandpapers from different countries may be graded differently. The United States uses a different grading system for grits than does Europe or Japan. Each system goes from coarse to fine. Europe uses the letter P in front of the grit number. Also, as you get into the higher-numbered and finer grits, the systems begin to diverge. Be sure to check your sandpaper manufacturer for comparison information as needed.

Sanding sponges, green scrubbing pads and steel wool, and polishing papers also come in handy in the studio. Sanding sponges are flexible, and they can be used wet or dry. You get a different grit on each side of the sponge. They are about ¼-inch thick and are pale gray in color. I don't like the thicker sponges that I've tried because I lose touch with the metal. Sanding sponges are more expensive than sandpaper, but they last a long time. They are a good choice when you need to reach into small, curved areas and for final finishing. They are available in packages of two, grouped as fine/medium or medium/coarse. (I like fine/medium.)

Green scrub pads and steel wool have an important place in metal finishing. A green scrubbing pad can be used wet, with Dawn detergent, to clean and degrease metal. Use it wet or dry to create a matte surface on metal. Steel wool comes in various grades, all the way to 0000 for a very fine, soft matte finish on metal. It can be used wet or dry, but it will rust. It contains oils, so don't use it when you need a grease-free surface for applying a patina, etching, or enameling.

Polishing papers are specialty products created to give metal a fine finish. They are available with a soft, fabric-like backing or a stiffer plastic backing. Polishing papers are graded in microns, which start out finer than most regular sandpapers and go finer still. You can use them wet or dry, but typically I use them dry. My favorite blue polishing paper is 9 microns, equivalent to 1200 grit in sandpaper, and is made by 3M. You can purchase a single sheet, multiple sheets, or assortments containing one each of the six types of polishing papers 3M makes.

Polishing compounds can be used with string to polish small, difficult to reach areas of your metal. This process is called thrumming. Simply cut a length of string and run it across a polishing compound, such as red rouge or Tripoli. These compounds are available in bars and containers. Your metal will need to be held in a clamp so you can use both hands to work the string in and out of your jewelry piece.

Pumice is another abrasive material that can be used to smooth and degrease metal. It is made from finely powdered volcanic rock. Pumice is typically used with water to make a paste that you apply to metal, rub, and rinse away. It's good for light sanding and scuffing of metal surfaces. It is also used as a preparation for etching or enameling on metal. You can often find it in a few different grades.

ARTISAN TIP

Any sandpaper, sanding sponge, or scrubbing pad can be cut with scissors into smaller sizes. These smaller sizes are more manageable for the purposes of this book. Be sure to use a permanent marker to write the grit on the back of any pieces of sandpaper you've cut. This label will save you from wondering exactly what you're using on your metal.

Understand the Three Major Types of Sanding

At various times during the process of making a piece of jewelry, you will want to smooth the surface of your metal by sanding it. The three major types of sanding differ based on when in the jewelry-making process you do them.

Right after you cut out a shape, you generally will want to remove sharp edges from the metal by filing them with your hand files. Then, you can do an initial sanding on your work by smoothing out any remaining rough edges with sandpaper. For this type of sanding, I use 220-grit, wet/dry sandpaper, and I use it dry.

If you are doing additional cutting, piercing, or soldering on your metal, you'll often need to sand before going further. For example, when you have sharp edges, bumps, or protrusions resulting from work performed after the initial sanding, you will need to sand again. In metalsmithing lingo, this activity is known as pre-polishing. Dry-sand your work using 220- or 320-grit, wet/dry sandpaper. Use it just enough to smooth the metal.

METAL MISHAP

If you have accidentally gouged your metal with a file or tool, you may need to file the area, and then sand it again. Always consider the surface of your metal (both sides) before you proceed to the next fabrication step. Ask yourself whether you'll be able to get back to the area to sand it later, or should you handle that job now?

Once you've finished making your jewelry, you might like a sanded finish instead of a polished finish. Finish sanding gives a softer, matte appearance to the final piece. It can also provide a compelling all-over scratchy appearance. The options vary with the type and grade of sandpaper you select. Once metal is smooth, you can go back to another grit of sandpaper or move to another polishing or surface treatment if you like.

Polish with Sandpaper

To sand to a final polish, use this sanding progression, which works for all types of metal:

1. Choose three grits of wet/dry sandpaper. Start with the most aggressive grit, which is the lowest number. I suggest using 220-grit sandpaper, then 320, and then 400 grit.

2. Sand in straight lines, moving back and forth across the surface of your metal.

3. Move to the next finer grit, sanding in the opposite direction (perpendicular to the previous direction). Sand until the marks from the first sanding disappears.

4. Use the final grit of sandpaper to finish polishing.

Burnishing

Burnishing is the activity of pressing or rubbing metal to give it a polished appearance. It's one more way to discover and exploit the plastic qualities of metal. Technically, what you're doing when burnishing metal is known as plastic deformation. This happens when two objects slide over one another, and each slightly deforms the other. In metalsmithing, you can do this in many ways with many things. In this section, you'll find out about how to achieve different results through burnishing and what to use to create them.

What You Can Achieve Through Burnishing

Burnishing removes small particles of metal. It's the finest form of sanding, really. Knowing how to apply this technique will give your work a refined appearance. A piece of jewelry that has been burnished properly and selectively will stand out from the crowd. You can take a piece of jewelry with a fine, all-over finish and rub the edges and high points with burnishing tools to smooth and brighten the metal.

Burnishing tools also are used when gemstones are set. Through burnishing, you can highlight folds, surface irregularities, and other areas of metal that you want to attract attention to. You can also use burnishing to remove small amounts of patina from select areas of metal, leaving other areas covered. This technique creates depth and surface interest.

What to Use as a Burnisher and How to Use It

The typical burnishing tool is made of stainless steel with a working end that tapers to a sharp point. However, the working end can be rounded, thick, thin, slightly curved, or short and squared.

Originally, I thought all burnishing tools were made of stainless steel, and that they were used strictly to smooth the thin metal that captured gemstones. But you can also find them in polished agate, tungsten carbide, brass, bronze, and plastic. Soon I learned that I could make my own burnishing tools from lots of different materials. And the tools can be used for a lot more than stone setting.

You can use these items to create your own burnishing tools:

- A toothbrush with the head cut off at an angle and sanded smooth.

- A large nail, with sharp edges filed smooth.

- A short length of wood dowel in whatever size needed.

- A length of polished brass or bronze shaped to a usable form.

- A piece of antler or horn. Mine was given to me years ago by a grizzled old metalsmith in Tennessee. I use it when I need something more refined and gentle than steel (Chapter 2 has a photograph of it).

It only takes a few moments to lop the head off of an old toothbrush, sand it, and create your own tool. Use the sanding progression detailed in the previous section to sand your tool to a 400-grit polish. If your burnisher becomes marred over time, you can cut a new face and repolish it or simply sand away the blemish. It will be good as new.

The actual activity of burnishing is simple. Take your preferred tool, apply it to the metal, and rub! The point of contact between the metal and your tool will be small. You can, by simply altering the angle of the burnisher ever so slightly, achieve many different looks. Altering the pressure will change things, too. While burnishing, be sure to prop your hands against the edge of your table or bench pin to hold the metal securely.

Suppose you have finished your work with a patina. If you take a burnishing tool to the edges of your metal and rub firmly, it will bring back a bit of sparkle. The patina is removed in a tiny area, and the bare metal is now highly polished. This one tiny detail elevates your work to pro status. Give it a try!

This steel burnishing tool helps brighten a copper cuff.

Joining Metal

In This Chapter

- How to make and use rivets
- How to make and use slots and tabs
- How and when to use glue
- What supplies are needed for soldering
- How to solder

There are three major ways to connect metal: cold connections, chemical bonds (also known as glue), and hot connections. This chapter presents key details about each one of these forms of connection and explains how to use them in your work. It includes information on the tools, materials, and other products to consider using in creating strong, lasting connections for your jewelry.

Rivets and Other Cold Connections

A *cold connection* is a means of connecting two or more items without the use of heat. To clarify, a torch setup may be used in the process of making a rivet or other cold connection component. Annealing, which requires heat, makes it easier to flare heavy wire or tubing into a rivet shape. But heat is not applied directly to the areas to be joined in a cold connection.

Rivets are one of the most popular and recognizable forms of cold connections. There are lots of different types of rivets used in an unbelievable variety of ways. Slots and tabs and jump rings are other forms of cold connection.

The greatest asset of cold connections is obvious—no soldering! For example, you can reach for a rivet when you have two pieces of metal that you want to connect, each with a different patina. If you heat up or try to solder these, the patina will be destroyed. If you are using paper, tin, fiber, wood, glass, beads, gems, or pearls in your jewelry, these must be joined to metal without heat, too. Very thin, delicate layers of metal or a very thick layer of metal with a thin layer on top can be safely joined together with rivets instead of risking a meltdown under the heat of a torch.

The process of making these cold connections involves techniques covered in other chapters. If you need tips on setting up a torch, see Chapter 2. Chapter 3 covers annealing, or softening metal. You'll also use a drill on your metal. If you need to brush up on drilling techniques, see Chapter 6. Jump rings are also used in cold connections, because they can be attached to jewelry without solder. Soldering makes for a stronger connection, though. Chapter 12 explains how to make jump rings.

A heavy wire rivet attaches a dog tag to this silver cuff bracelet.

The two layers of this copper cuff are connected with silver rivets.

(© Paul D'Andrea)

Making and Using Rivets

Making rivets is easy and approachable in the home studio. To make rivets, you'll need the following basic tools and supplies:

- Riveting hammer, ball-peen hammer, or goldsmith's hammer
- Drill bit set and hand or power drill
- Lubricant for drill bit
- Center punch
- Steel bench block
- Jeweler's saw and number 2/0 or 3/0 blades
- Metal shears
- Small, round needle file; pointed burnisher or scribe; or broach set
- Number 2 flat hand file or whatever file you have
- Flat-nosed pliers
- Torch setup for annealing metal
- Wire or tubing for rivet-making
- Fine-point permanent marker
- Safety goggles

Key elements in riveting are fit and finish. The rivet must have a snug fit inside a hole of the proper size, and it must not be too tall or too short. Thicker wire—12, 14, or 16 gauge—is easier to work with when you are making wire rivets. When in doubt, go with thicker wire. Tubing is stronger than wire, so you can go thinner with tubing.

To make rivets, you start out with wire or tubing that is too long, insert it into the drilled hole, and then cut it to the right length. To get a properly sized hole for your rivet, select a drill bit slightly smaller than the size hole you need. You can use a round file, scribe with a tapered point, or a broach to enlarge holes until the rivet fits snugly.

After you insert the rivet, you need to widen the ends of the rivet so that it stays in place. *Upsetting* the rivet takes a bit of practice. Using small, measured tapping is better than a few hard hammer blows. Work the piece gradually, turning it over often to hammer the rivet on both sides.

DEFINITION

Upsetting a rivet means hammering each end of the rivet to widen it and keep the rivet in place.

Making Wire Rivets

A wire rivet is a common type of rivet that is used to join two or more metal or nonmetal items. Wire is inserted into a snug hole, cut to length, and hammered to widen, or upset, the ends.

To make a wire rivet, follow these steps:

1. Select the wire and the drill bit. Measure the thickness of your wire and find a matching drill bit or one that is slightly smaller. Use a longer wire than you need. If you can't cut it with your wire shears, make a right-sized hole in your bench pin, put the wire in it, and saw it off with the saw held sideways.

2. Anneal the wire.

3. Mark, dent, and drill one hole in each layer to be joined, one layer at a time.

Hold the jeweler's saw sideways when you saw a wire.

4. Put your layers together, and work the wire through the opening. If the fit is too tight, use a pointed scribe or burnishing tool to enlarge the hole. Or use a small round file, being careful not to wrench the file and break it off in the hole. You also can use a broach to shave off tiny amounts of metal. Twist it gently around the inside of the hole.

> **METAL MISHAP**
>
> If the hole becomes too large, you can close it back up a little bit by hammering gently around the opening. Use the ball end of a ball-peen hammer or a small, round punch with a hammer. If this doesn't work, you'll need to use thicker wire. If you don't have thicker wire you may be able to use a washer or disc. Cut two for each hole, and place them on either side of the opening.

5. Once you have a good fit for the rivet, cut off the excess wire. Leave a small amount of wire on either side of your project. File the end of the wire flat.

6. Place your project on the bench block. Make sure some wire is sticking up on both sides of the layers. The rivet should make good contact with the bench block. Hold the layers slightly above the bench block. Upset the rivet by hammering it lightly a few times.

7. Turn the metal over and hammer the other side lightly a few times. Repeat until the metal is flared and fits snugly.

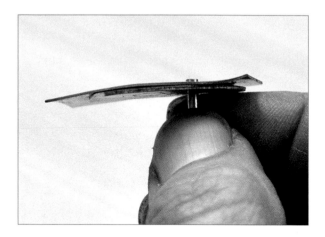

This wire rivet fits in its hole, and one end of it has been cut to an appropriate length.

The back side of a pendant shows the detail of a completed wire rivet.

(© Paul D'Andrea)

Making Tube Rivets

A tube rivet is another common type of rivet in which a length of tubing is used in the same way as a wire is used in a wire rivet. The tubing can be cut or filed around the edge to add to the design. A tube rivet is a bit easier to set than a wire rivet, due to the vertical strength of the tube. There is also something to be said for the visual interest of the negative space created by the hole in the tubing.

To make a tube rivet, you need the same tools and materials as for wire rivets. In addition, you need the following items:

- Tube-cutting jig, tube-holding pliers, or a right-sized hole in your bench pin

- Tubing in the size you need

- Bench pin

To make a tube rivet, follow these steps:

1. Select a drill bit that is slightly smaller than the diameter of your tube. Put it in your drill and lubricate it.

This silver pendant features tube rivets.

2. Precut the tubing using a tube-cutting jig or tube-holding/cutting pliers and a jeweler's saw with a 3/0 blade. Rest the jig or pliers against your bench pin for support. Go slowly while cutting tubing. Cut it just slightly longer than needed for your project. You'll file it down once it is in place.

3. Anneal the cut tubing if you have a torch setup. This step is important with thick tubing or when you have delicate materials to rivet and don't want to subject your work to many blows from the hammer. Take care when annealing tubing, as it heats up quickly.

4. Mark, dent, and drill one hole in each layer to be joined, one layer at a time.

5. Work the tubing into the rivet hole. It can be helpful to place the tubing on the end of a scribe until you can get it into the rivet hole. Use a flat file to file down excess tubing. Allow a small amount of tubing to protrude above and below the metal being riveted.

6. Place your project on the bench block. Make sure some metal is protruding from both sides. Place the center punch into the opening of the tube, and tap the punch with a hammer two or three times. This will start to flare the tubing.

Prop the tube-cutting jig against the bench pin when cutting tubing with a jeweler's saw.

Use a dapping punch to flare a tube rivet.

ARTISAN TIP

If you have a series of rivets to create, start by drilling one hole in each layer. With these holes in alignment, mark the topmost layer with the rest of the rivet locations. Drill the holes in the top layer only. Place the top layer over the next layer. Line up the two original holes, and rivet those together. Choose a hole opposite the first one. Using your marked pattern to guide you, drill the second hole and set the rivet for that hole. Once the layers are stabilized, you can drill the rest of the holes, using your pattern as a guide.

7. Flip the work over and repeat this on the other side. Continue until the punch will no longer flare the metal.

8. Switch to the ball end of a small ball-peen hammer to complete the riveting.

Customize Your Rivets

You can finish off your rivets by filing and sanding them, but you may find that, with practice, this step becomes unneeded.

Here are a few additional ways to trick out your rivets:

Add spacers. Place a length of tubing between two or more elements. Slide the rivet through the tube, leaving a little bit of metal protruding from each end of the tube. Upset the rivet as usual. The spacer adds strength and a dimensional quality to your work.

Decorate your rivet. Solder a metal cut-out to a piece of wire or tubing to add a decorative element. Use the completed decorative rivet the same as you would a wire rivet.

Hide your rivet or make it flush. Countersink the drilled hole by partially drilling it, using a larger drill bit. This creates a beveled cutout. Insert a wire and hammer it to fill this opening. Then file any protruding wire down to the level of the surrounding metal, rendering it all but invisible.

Make rivets with flaps. Splitting a rivet head into an X shape with a jeweler's saw adds a decorative touch. It also reduces the amount of hammering needed. This technique works best with tubing, but you also can use heavy-gauge wire, such as 10 or 12 gauge. If you need to anneal the rivets, wait until after you have cut them or they'll bend while being cut.

Mark the X cutting pattern on your rivet with a fine-point permanent marker. Use your jeweler's saw to cut the rivet in quadrants. Stop cutting when you reach the center of the tube or wire, and move to the next quadrant. You can insert the resulting rivet in the rivet hole and pull it open with pliers. Then gently hammer it open. You can create a much longer rivet in this way. This technique works well on very delicate items or as a way to create visual interest.

Add washers. Washers are sometimes used in addition to rivets for additional security or decorative elements. You can make these or purchase small ones at hardware stores or

A flap rivet is flared with the ball end of a hammer.

online. They come in handy with fabric and leather, as these can stretch and pull away from the rivet. A washer on either side of the material will prevent that. To make a washer with a disc cutter, make the small hole in your metal first. Then position the metal to create the larger hole.

Make nails. Use a torch to melt one end of a piece of wire into a ball. Place the wire in a small vice or pair of pliers and tap down the balled end of the wire. Release the grip and turn the rivet around to the other side. Tap the balled end a few times to get an even nail head. You also can hold the wire in a ring clamp and hammer it with a riveting hammer to spread the end, creating a nail head. Use the nail the same way you would use a wire rivet.

Create articulating rivets. Articulating rivets are rivets that move. You can create this style of rivet by adding a temporary spacer during the riveting process and then removing the spacer after the rivet is set. My favorite way to do this is to use the fake credit cards from offers I get in the mail. Cut these into rectangular strips with a *V* shape in one end. The *V* needs to snug up to the rivet. This spacer is placed in between the layers, with enough sticking out to facilitate its removal when you're done setting the rivet.

Two items are riveted with plastic in between to create an articulating rivet.

A little bit of time spent with some scrap metal, found objects, and some wire or tubing will have you making remarkable rivets in record time.

Making and Using Slots and Tabs

Slots and tabs are another type of cold connection. In this type of connection a pierced opening, or *slot*, matches a protrusion, or *tab*. The tab is inserted in the slot and bent over with fingers, pliers, or with a hammer to connect two areas or secure found objects.

Slots and tabs come in handy for creating architecture and dimension in your work. Like rivets, you don't need heat to join slots and tabs. But you may need to anneal the metal after you've made the tabs. This will make them easier to bend over.

> **ARTISAN TIP**
>
> You can take a single sheet of metal, and cut slots in one end and tabs in the other. Anneal the whole piece, and bend the ends around a dowel rod until they meet. Insert the tabs and bend them over for a cylinder-shaped object.

Glues

Different types of glues and epoxies create chemical bonds. These are used to join surfaces, or to attach pearls and found objects to jewelry items. Glues can be used to adhere two parts together or as a holding or sealing medium. Some things are too difficult to connect using any other method.

In my early years of metalsmithing, I thought glues were bad. Over time, I learned the value in using them, and have tried many types of chemical bonds and methods of bonding. For instance, it's easier and feels more secure to put a drop of epoxy on a well-made pearl peg versus pushing the pearl onto a friction-mount peg and hoping it'll hold forever.

Glues can also be a temporary means of holding things together. For example, when soldering many small parts, you can use a drop of cyanoacrylate gel glue (such as Super Glue) to hold things together until soldering is complete. With rubber cement, you can adhere a paper pattern directly to metal. After you no longer need the pattern, you can easily remove the rubber cement. And finally, you can use certain two-part or resin epoxies to create a thick, crystal-clear coating over an image contained in a bezel cup. You also can use it as a carrier for various mix-ins, such as sand, confetti, and coloring agents. Be sure to look for brands that dry crystal-clear when cured.

Creating a chemical bond with glue requires just a little bit of preparation. Make sure the metal is absolutely clean and dry. The surface must be grease-free and dust-free for the glue to hold. It helps to have some "tooth" for the glue to grab onto. You can create this by lightly roughing up the surface of your metal with 400-grit wet/dry sandpaper or by scoring your work with files. Use denatured alcohol or acetone on the surface for pristinely clean metal.

Glues aren't something you'll reach for every day, but a handful of tried-and true glues do come in handy. These often show up in the well-rounded metalsmith's toolkit. In the following sections, I tell you about the glues I like and how to use them. You can decide for yourself if you want to add them to your beginning metalsmith's toolbox.

Rubber Cement

Use rubber cement to stick patterns to clean, dust-free metal surfaces. Apply a thin, even coat to both your metal surface and your pattern. Allow the rubber cement to become tacky, which takes a few minutes, depending on the temperature and humidity in your studio. Then apply the pattern and gently smooth any air bubbles with your fingers. Allow it to dry before sawing or piercing your design. When you are finished cutting your design, roll the pattern off of your metal using your fingers or soak the metal briefly in soapy water and remove the pattern with a green scrubbing pad.

Two-Part Epoxy

Two-part epoxies consist of a resin and a hardener. My favorite, Devcon 2-Ton 30-Minute Epoxy, dries crystal clear in 30 minutes and is fully cured in about 6 hours. To mix the epoxy, use a piece of paper torn from a file folder or use a paper plate. Squeeze equal-sized drops of resin and hardener onto the paper, side by side. Using a toothpick, mix them together for one full minute, timed by the clock. Apply it to metal that's been cleaned with denatured alcohol.

When using epoxy to set pearls or found objects onto pegs, I make dents with pliers or file small cuts in the pegs. This gives a place for the epoxy to grab onto. I then apply the epoxy to the tip of the peg and allow it to drip down to the base of the peg. I add the pearl or found object, and hold it in place for a full minute. Then I wipe away any excess using a clean piece of paper toweling dampened with denatured alcohol. I prop the piece so the object remains upright and leave it overnight to cure. (Chapter 11 has more information about how to set gemstones and found objects.)

This Walk in the Woods pendant is a box with a prism glass cover, and inside is a twig set on a peg with epoxy.

Hot Connections

Hands down, soldering is the aspect of metalsmithing that brings the most questions—and the biggest fears. This section provides step-by-step instructions on how to solder your work. Successful soldering only requires a willingness to learn, a bit of equipment, and some space around you to do it safely. Everything else you can learn by doing.

What Is Solder?

To solder is to use heat and a compatible metal alloy with a slightly lower melting point to join metal. Solders themselves are alloys, or mixtures of metals, designed to melt before the metals to be joined. Melting solder flows between close-fitting seams and into the crystalline structure of the metal, creating a strong, secure join. A good solder join is as strong as the metal it has joined together. You'll be able to solder a good join or fuse metal, too, using the tips in this section.

Solders are available in many metals (including gold and copper), but my focus throughout this book is on silver solder for the purposes of soldering both base and precious metals. Silver solder is flexible in that you can use it on any silver alloy and copper, brass, nickel silver, or bronze. If you are soldering gold to silver, you can use silver solder for that, too. Just don't use welding solder or the solders from the hardware store!

Silver solders have different melting points, based upon the percentage of silver that was used in the alloy to make them. Solders with the highest percentages of silver melt at the highest temperatures. The higher the silver content of your solder, the better it will match silver projects. You won't be able to detect a solder seam color difference with higher temperature solders. Lower silver content solders may flow more easily, but the color match isn't as good. The most commonly used solders are easy, medium, and hard, with easy melting at the lowest temperature and hard melting at the highest. Other solder alloys are available with even higher and lower melting points, but I'll concentrate on using easy, medium, and hard solders.

METAL MISHAP

To prevent mix-ups, store your silver solders apart from silver metal. There's no easy way to tell the difference between silver and silver solder! Keep them in well-marked containers, and write the grade of solder on both the solder and the storage container. Keep solders obtained from different manufacturers in separate containers, too, even if the solder is the same grade. Different suppliers have their own grading system for solders. A hard solder from one manufacturer may melt at a slightly higher or lower melting point than a hard solder from another manufacturer. Initially, I'd recommend purchasing your solder through a single supplier until you are comfortable with soldering.

Solder is available in sheet, wire, and lower-melting point paste. I focus on using sheet and wire solders. There is no magic in choosing one over the other. Sheets are cut into smaller pieces, called *pallions* or chips. Wire solder is sold in coils of thin wire and also may be cut into smaller chips.

Solder must be clean before cutting it and using it. Do this by folding a piece of 400-grit wet/dry sandpaper in half and drawing the sheet or wire through the sandpaper to clean it. I store a piece of sandpaper with my solder packets just for this purpose. You can also put tarnished solder into the pickle pot to clean it. Leave it for five minutes, neutralize it, and then rinse and dry it. Hold it by the edges to keep it clean.

To cut solder, take your clean solder sheet or wire and cut it into small chips, about ⅛-inch (3 millimeters) square. You can make a handy tray to catch the chips as you cut them. Cut a rectangle of paper and fold each end a half-inch (1 centimeter) away from the edges. Write the type of solder directly on the tray. Make separate trays as needed.

For sheet solder, start a cut at the short end using sharp scissors, traveling parallel to the long edge. Cut one or two of these strips about 2 inches (5 centimeters) long, but don't cut them off of the sheet completely. Leave them attached, creating a fringe. Snip into the fringe. Let the chips fall into the container. Hold your hands at an angle, so the chips fall into the tray rather than spraying all over the place. Don't touch the chips if you can help it. Wire solder is easy to cut. Just cut it over your tray and allow the pieces to fall in.

Cut sheet solder into a paper tray to contain the chips.

ARTISAN TIP

Cut chips only as you need them. It's easy to clean tarnish and dirt from full sheets of solder. It's impractical to do this with tiny chips. If you have tiny solder chips that are tarnished, it's best to start over with fresh solder. Dirty solder won't flow.

What Supplies Do I Need for Soldering?

In Chapter 2, you learned about torches and torch setups. You also learned about the items you'll need to set up a torch workstation, along with a safe torch practices checklist. Any torch you select requires the same basic setup and safety precautions, including a fire extinguisher and good ventilation.

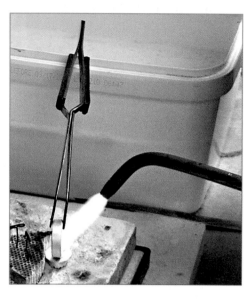

I often use a combination of surfaces when soldering. For basic soldering, a Solderite pad or fire brick works great. You can push t-pins into its surface to hold things in place. You can place them on a turntable that rotates your work as you solder. When you want a perfectly hard, flat surface, use a honeycomb surface. The holes facilitate even heating and allow you to hold parts firmly in place with t-pins that anchor down into the surface below.

The cross-lock tweezers are holding a ring in place during soldering.

Sometimes you'll need additional ways to hold things when soldering. Cross-lock tweezers come in handy for holding things in place. Binding wire can be wrapped around metal and turned with pliers to create a tightening kink. You also can cut it to make props to suspend your project or bend it into clips to hold small items together. A stack of nickels come in handy as props, too.

All metal items used as props will draw heat away from your solder join and create what's known as a *heat sink*. Be aware of this when heating metal and props. Keep flux and solder away from props and binding wire, too, because they could become soldered to your work. In addition, props, binding wire, and steel tools all contain iron and will react when in contact with the pickle solution, depositing a copper plating on everything in the pot. So keep them out of the pickle pot. Use copper tongs when adding or removing items from the pickle solution.

DEFINITION

A **heat sink** is a substance that absorbs heat. Anything metal used to hold or prop your work during soldering will create a heat sink. That means heat will be drawn to that area of metal and away from areas to be soldered. This will require you to adjust the amount of heat and length of time needed to bring everything up to proper soldering temperature.

Flux is used in soldering to keep oxides from forming and allow the solder to flow. It is applied to metal as a liquid or paste and provides visual cues when heated. When torch heat is applied indirectly around a fluxed area, the heat makes the water in the flux bubble and boil away. Then the flux turns a pasty white. As the metal heats up, the flux changes consistency, becoming thick and clear. The flame is then moved in close to complete soldering.

White paste flux is painted on copper with strips of easy (left), medium (middle), and hard (right) silver solder.

The paste flux turns white from indirect heat.

The white paste flux is heated to clear, and the solder melts.

How Do I Solder?

The general process for soldering is that you apply flux and solder to metal, heat it until the water in the flux boils off, and then melt the solder. The whole operation from start to finish takes mere minutes. Obviously, there are some details around doing that!

Before you fire up the torch, you need to prepare your materials:

1. Check your connections. Make sure that all the pieces and parts of your jewelry project fit together well. Hold your work up to the light to inspect for gaps. File, sand, or bend the metal until you get a good fit.

2. Clean your metal. Clean all parts of metal to be soldered using a good degreasing detergent, such as Dawn, and a green scrubbing pad or a brass brush and water. Rinse and dry. Some parts may be better cleaned by using sandpaper. Once your metal is clean, hold it by the edges to avoid touching areas to be soldered.

3. Prepare your solder. Choose the right solder for the job, starting with hard solder and working your way through medium and easy solder for subsequent operations. Cut your solder into tiny pallions, letting them fall onto a small paper tray or container. Mark your container with the type of solder that's in it.

4. Apply flux. Use a flux brush if using paste flux, and apply a thin, even coat to areas to be soldered. Use a heavier coat on thicker metal and copper, as it oxidizes rapidly.

5. Prepare soldering props. Hold your work in place at the soldering station with t-pins, "shelves" of nickels, or binding wire. Only use these as needed and remove them before pickling.

6. Choose your torch. If you have multiple torch options or torch tips, choose a torch or tip size that relates to the size of your work. A long seam on a large piece of metal requires more heat and a larger torch tip to produce a flame that is sufficient to reach the proper soldering temperature. Micro torches can handle soldering jobs on jewelry items 1 inch (2.5 centimeters) across or smaller. Larger items usually need a bigger, hotter flame.

Now you are ready to solder:

1. Light the torch. Hold it in your nondominant hand. Hold your soldering pick in your dominant hand. Use the tip of the flame to warm the solder surface around the project.

2. Melt the flux. With the torch flame pointed straight down towards the flameproof work surface, begin moving the flame around the edges of the metal, getting just close enough to make the flux bubble. This might make the solder move out of place. If it does, reposition it with your pick.

3. Move the heat closer, and keep it moving. Use the hottest part of the flame now, which is the part just outside of the inner deep-blue cone, and focus on heating the larger mass of your "parent" metal. (This is the metal to which smaller pieces are soldered.)

4. Watch for the flux to turn clear. When it does, your metal is near the point at which it will melt the solder. Solder flows like water and flashes silver when it melts.

Silver solder flows on the seam of a ring.

5. Move the flame across the parent metal in the direction you want the solder to flow, and your solder will follow along. Keep the heat focused mostly upon the parent metal to prevent unintentional melting of smaller pieces that are being soldered.

6. As soon as you see that solder has flowed all along your join, remove the flame.

7. Cool your metal to black heat. When the metal loses its red color and turns black, quench it in water. Make sure to allow large, flat works to air-cool completely before quenching to inhibit warping.

8. Pickle, neutralize, and rinse your metal.

Congratulations, you've soldered!

Closely check your solder join to be sure it "took." Use soapy water and a green scrubbing pad or a brass brush to remove the film from your metal. Rinse your item again, dry it, and proceed.

What Are the Types of Solder Operations and When Do I Use Them?

There are five main types of soldering operations: chip, sweat, pick, stick, and paste. Chip and sweat soldering are the most common types of soldering needed in beginning metalsmithing.

In chip soldering, tiny chips are placed between pieces of metal, creating a bridge. This type of soldering works well for rings, bezels, and large seams. To chip-solder, flux all of the areas to be soldered. Position the solder chips at an angle to lean against the two pieces being soldered or to create tiny bridges where two flat pieces meet. Use fine-point tweezers, or a pick you have touched into the flux jar, to help you pick up and place the chips.

> **ARTISAN TIP**
>
> Heating solder directly won't make it flow! It's important to heat the area around the metal to allow the flux to warm slowly and bubble gently.

The sweat soldering method is handy for soldering a small item to a larger one by melting solder on the smaller item and placing the items together to complete soldering. It also keeps solder contained to the areas where it's needed. To sweat-solder, follow these steps:

1. Place the pieces to be soldered side by side. Flux both pieces.

2. Apply solder chips to smaller piece(s). Heat all pieces until flux finishes bubbling and turns white. Reposition chips of solder with your soldering pick as needed.

3. Focus the heat near the smaller piece(s), just until the solder slumps. Turn the small piece over using your fine-point tweezers, and place it on top of the larger piece.

4. Move the flame around the large piece, concentrating the heat on the larger mass of metal. The smaller piece may float a bit. Use your pick to guide the piece into position if needed. If the pick sticks to your work, move the flame closer, and the heat will release it.

5. When the solder flows, the small piece will settle down onto the larger one. You may see a flash of silver between the small and large pieces. At this point, remove the heat.

Chips of solder are propped around a silver bezel cup.

In this sweat soldering setup, the larger pieces have been heated until the fluxed areas turned white. The two smaller pieces contain chips of solder.

The pick, stick, and paste methods are examples of other soldering operations. The pick method is often used for soldering lots of jump rings, chain, or for production work. A hot solder pick is used to pick up a small chip of solder. The work is heated, and the melted ball of solder from the pick is transferred to the work.

In the stick method, wire solder or a long, thin strip of sheet solder is touched to metal that has reached soldering temperature. This method works well for long solder seams. Care must be taken to not melt too much solder onto the seam.

In the paste method, the solder has been mixed with a carrier and loaded into syringes. Usually lower-temperature solders are used. This method is most often used in low-temperature production work.

What Else Should I Know About Soldering?

In your quest for a perfect solder seam, you might need some extra expert advice. I have tested every technique listed in this section to make sure it works.

If you have a large piece to solder, prop it up so heat can reach underneath. Place a metal mesh trivet on top of your heatproof surface and under large pieces. Or make a coil of binding wire by wrapping wire around a dowel rod, pulling the rod free, and twisting the ends of the wire together. Both of the aforementioned props will create a heat sink, so heat them up while you are heating your parent metal. Also, place broken bits of ceramic honeycomb block on top of your heatproof surface. Set your metal on top, so heat can travel under and around the broken pieces. An advantage to this setup is that you can anchor the honeycomb pieces to the subsurface with t-pins.

Sometimes you don't want solder to flow into certain areas. To keep it out, use dirt or grease to prevent it. Anti-flux agents are incredibly messy and often get themselves into areas where they are not wanted or needed. Dirt works better.

You may resolder using the same grade of solder multiple times. Although it's safe to do three soldering operations using hard, medium, and then easy solder, eventually you'll want to create work that requires many more soldered joins. Start with hard solder and use it for as many operations as possible, if not all operations. Only move to lower melting-point solders when necessary.

You can thin solder sheets and wire for your more delicate soldering operations or for use on long seams. Do this by hammering the solder or by running it through a rolling mill.

Don't solder when you're tired, angry, hungry, or 10 minutes before you have to leave the room (or the end of the class). There's a certain unexplainable mojo that must be maintained when you're in the soldering mode.

METAL MISHAP

Heating the metal for too long can burn off the flux and allow oxides to form. This will look like black glue or flaky black dirt. This coating won't allow solder to flow. If this happens, quench, pickle, and reapply flux and solder to your metal.

What Are the Basic Steps for Soldering?

Review this short list right before soldering to prompt you to recall the needed steps:

1. Clean it. Have very clean metal and solder.

2. Fit it. Make sure pieces fit together well.

3. Flux it. Apply flux in an even coat.

4. Solder it. Add solder and apply heat. Get in and get out!

5. Quench, pickle, neutralize, rinse, and dry.

CHAPTER

9

Creating Surface Textures and Impressions

In This Chapter

- Hammer marks
- Hand tool textures
- Power tool textures
- Customized metal stamps
- Steps for etching
- Uses for a rolling mill and a car

Surface textures and impressions made on metal offer a way to communicate a message, to evoke a response in the viewer, or just to add beauty. Fortunately for today's metalsmith, there are hundreds of easy ways to get some surface interest going on metal.

Textures are created on metal through the use of varying degrees of applied force, which means to displace metal through hammering or stamping or to remove some metal as in engraving, or with chemicals. On the low-tech end of things, you can use hammers, stamps, punches, and gravers. These tools are available for purchase or you can make your own. If you introduce power to the mix, hundreds more options are available. In this chapter, I explain how to use the flexible shaft machine to make all manner of marks on your metal. You also get detailed instructions on how to etch copper and brass. Grab some scrap metal to test these techniques, and let's get started!

Creating Textures with Hammers

The beauty of hammer marks is one of the many surface design options available to you. Every hammer has a head with two faces, and each face produces a different texture. The weight and length of the hammer head will have an impact on the impressions it makes. Although any hammer can be used to create texture on the surface of metal, this isn't always the best use for every hammer. Certain hammers were meant for certain jobs.

This copper cuff bracelet has a hammered texture.

ARTISAN TIP

Before hammering your metal, be sure to anneal it. Heating the metal with a torch and quenching it in water or allowing it to air-cool will soften it and make it a lot easier to move with the force of your hammer blows.

From left to right, these hammers are ball-peen, goldsmith's, planishing/forming, raising, embossing, forging, and rawhide.

My favorite hammers are the planishing and forging hammers. A planishing hammer may be rounded on one side and flat on the other, or both sides may be flat. The flat side smoothes metal, and the rounded side provides more texture. The rounded face of my planishing hammer creates classic hammer impressions that look like little round dimples. The head of a forging hammer is wedge-shaped with one large, broad face and one smaller, rectangular face. Think of a blacksmith's hammer. The narrow, rectangular face of my 1,000-gram forging hammer creates the most wonderful line textures. I use these hammers on any size jewelry. I have purchased many hammers, including the specialty types listed below, but come back to these two proven winners.

Here are some other commonly used hammers, the jobs they do, and marks they create:

Ball-peen. This general purpose hammer is for flattening, shaping, and texturing. One side is rounded, and the other side is flat. It looks similar to a planishing hammer, but the head is usually more compact.

Raising. This hammer forms metal without thinning it. Heads are available in wide, rectangular shapes; smaller wedge-shapes; or broad, bowed shapes. Many sizes are available. Look for thinner, wedge-shaped heads to create dramatic, raised-line textures.

Chasing. This hammer has a flared, flat face with a small peen on the opposite end. The flared face is meant to strike punches. You can use the ball end to create texture.

Bordering. This hammer creates an interesting texture similar to a forging hammer's smaller rectangular face.

Embossing. The two tiny rounded ends of this specialty hammer create deep dimples in metal.

Making Scratch Textures

Scratch textures are simple to apply to metal. You can make them using supplies from your basic toolkit or from household items. They can also be applied using power tools, such as the flexible shaft machine. Note that it's not necessary to anneal metal before using hand tools or power tools to texture it.

Hand Tool Textures

The following tools offer a low-tech way to quickly create a scratch texture on your metal:

Nail. Drag it across the surface or use an up-and-down tapping motion to stipple tiny dents in your metal. Larger sizes are easier to hold than smaller sizes.

Burnishing tool. The point of this tool can dig deep into metal. Use it to draw randomly in any design you like, create swirls, or drag lines in your metal.

Brass or steel brush. Use this with some soapy water to create an all-over soft matte effect.

Green scrubbing pad. Use this either wet or dry with circular motions to create a subtle swirled effect.

Steel wool. Use 0000 very fine steel wool, and use it dry, to create a soft, swirled matte effect. Afterwards, rinse your metal in clean water to remove any steel wool bits, and then dry it.

ARTISAN TIP

A clean, sanded, smooth finish on your metal helps any texture you apply to stand out more. If you decide to sand first, use a progression of 200-, 320-, and 400-grit wet/dry sandpaper on your metal until it's as smooth and shiny as you like. Then proceed to add texture with one of the methods in this chapter.

To enhance the texture further, consider an applied patina, such as liver of sulfur (see Chapter 10 for information on patinas). Or you can polish the surface of your metal with a piece of denim (like your blue jeans) or with 600-grit wet/dry sandpaper.

Power Tool Textures

Power tools create textures that would be cumbersome or impossible to create with hand tools. My favorite power tool is the flexible shaft machine, or *flex shaft*. The adjustable chuck handpiece accompanying the flex shaft allows for multiple burs and bits to be used. The possibilities are endless.

Experimentation is important in understanding how a texture will work on metal. Practice making textures on a piece of copper. You can draw a design onto the metal with a fine-point permanent marker. Or you can wing it and experiment with an all-over surface texture or random application. The choice is yours.

To create textures on metal using the flex shaft, start with whatever burs you have available to you. Then follow these steps:

1. Put on your safety goggles.

2. Select your bur and chuck it into the handpiece. Tighten it firmly.

This texture bur is being chucked into a flex shaft handpiece.

> **ARTISAN TIP**
>
> A low-tech power tool option you can use to create surface interest is the electric pen. It's a simple handheld unit with a pointed metal tip. Electric pens are available at most hardware stores. Most machines come with a dial that allows you to increase the vibrating speed of the tip. I use this machine to sign my name to my work.

3. Place your metal on the bench pin. Firmly hold the metal down with your nondominant hand, propping your hand against the bench pin to steady it.

4. Holding the handpiece in your dominant hand, start the motor slowly and apply the bur to your metal. Don't press down hard.

5. Slowly lift and lower the bur to the metal until you achieve the design you're after.

Stamping Metal

The three main types of stamps for the jewelry maker are alphanumeric, decorative, and hallmark. Alphanumeric and decorative stamps for metal make it easy to create jewelry with sayings, names, initials, or established images. This type of jewelry has exploded in popularity in recent years. Hallmark stamps are the behind-the-scenes stamp. They serve to impress precious metal jewelry with quality marks.

The number of commercially available stamps in varying images, font styles, and sizes is truly staggering. It's easy to find stamps and their related equipment, which includes a simple steel or brass hammer and a flat steel block. These offer so many ways to make a personal mark or statement on metal. This section explains how to use these stamps in your work.

Gathering Your Tools and Preparing Your Metal

Stamps are usually made from a 3- to 4-inch (8 to 10 centimeters) long piece of tool steel. The steel is specially heat treated, or hardened, to give you many years of good, crisp impressions. That is to say, it will as long as you take simple steps to prepare your metal and use your tools properly.

The first step in stamping is to gather your tools:

Stamps

Copper

Hammer (unpolished utility or brass)

Steel block or anvil

Goggles

Work gloves

Optional: Torch setup

> **ARTISAN TIP**
>
> Hallmarking precious metal originated in the United Kingdom around 1300. A regulating body called an Assay Office was set up in order to test and hallmark items made of precious metal. This practice began with silver and today encompasses gold and other precious metals. Interestingly, jewelry makers in the United States are not required to send items to a regulating office for precious metal verification and stamping. If you reside in the United States, however, it's still a good idea to both sign and hallmark your precious metal jewelry items.

To stamp metal, you need stamps, a steel block, a piece of copper, and a brass mallet.

> **SAFE 'SMITHING**
>
> Striking steel with the flesh of your hand so close by can be nerve wracking. That's why you need to wear goggles and gloves. You also need to keep children, the elderly, and pets out of the area. Steel stamps or hammers can shatter and fly long distances without warning.

Anneal both your practice copper scrap metal and your project metal. A stamped or punched impression is more deeply described into annealed metal, because the metal is soft. Take a few moments to review the annealing procedures in Chapter 3 if you need information on annealing the different types of metal. Quench and dry your metal.

When using stamps on your jewelry project, you need to lay your project flat on a steel block. Flatten your metal if needed. Straighten and smooth any bends or bumps with your fingers, or very gently with a rawhide mallet. Keep in mind that too much mallet action will work-harden your metal. You can bend, form, and solder your work after you stamp it. Formed areas can crumple under the stamp or a stray hammer blow, so it's best to do forming after stamping.

Creating the Impression

With your tools laid out and your metal ready, follow these steps to create a stamped impression:

1. Place your annealed metal on the steel bench block.

2. Holding the stamp in your dominant hand, position it wherever you would like the impression.

3. Rock the stamp a bit to make sure it is in full contact with your metal.

4. Look at the striking area of the stamp. Don't look at your thumb. The hammer falls where your eyes are looking.

An impression of a flower has been stamped on this copper.

Strike the stamp with a hammer to create an impression on your metal.

> **ARTISAN TIP**
>
> Don't use wood underneath your metal. It is too soft to create a clean impression. Instead, it will leave an undesirable dimple.

5.   Strike your stamp firmly, directly on the head. The action is more a good tap than a hard blow.

6.   Without lifting the stamp, rock it just a touch to one side and strike again.

7.   Rock the stamp to each of the four sides and strike it.

The rock, strike, rock method works well for me. Try it a few times until you get good results. Stamps with larger surface areas almost always work better with the rock, strike, rock method.

The drawback with this method is that several small blows can sometimes give you a double impression. To counter that, you can try the one big blow method. This method means you strike the metal squarely and very firmly only one time. A drawback of the one big blow method is it can make the metal jump and give you a partial impression. I recommend experimenting with both methods on a variety of stamps.

Etching

Another option for surface design is etching. Some very detailed results can be achieved with this process. Etched metal can be used in projects just the same as any other metal. Just be sure not to file or sand it too much, or the detail will be lost.

In general, etched metal is partially covered with a *resist*, which protects that part of the metal from the etching chemical. The etching chemical is known as an *etchant* or *mordant*. The uncovered part of the metal is corroded. This action is known as the *bite*. The chemicals used, how they are mixed, and how they are neutralized depends upon the kind of metal being etched. In this section, I tell you how to etch metal using ferric chloride, a common etching mordant.

> **DEFINITIONS**
>
> A **resist** is a coating applied to metal that withstands the effects of chemicals. An **etchant** is a chemical used to produce a design on the surface of metal. A **mordant** is any chemical used in the metal etching process.

Handling Chemicals Safely

As with any metalworking process, safety is important when using etching chemicals. Read the labels carefully to determine how to neutralize any chemicals you'll be using. In some cases, baking soda works. In the case of ferric chloride, ammonia is the neutralizing agent.

Be sure to dispose of used chemicals properly. You will probably need to take spent ferric chloride to a hazardous waste facility. Ferric chloride also stains everything. Protect your skin and work surfaces accordingly.

When working with any chemicals, you must prepare yourself with the following safety precautions:

- Good ventilation
- Apron (fabric or chemical-resistant material)
- Gloves (chemical resistant)
- Goggles
- Respirator
- Fresh water
- Nonmetal containers for mixing
- Neutralizing solutions

> **SAFE 'SMITHING**
>
> "Acid to water, do as you ought-er." Hopefully this funny adage will stick in your mind to help you remember that you must always add acid to water when mixing chemicals. Adding water to acid can create heat and splatter the acid into the air.

Gathering Supplies and Applying a Design

The etching chemical used in this chapter is ferric chloride, also known as iron chloride. Its vapors contain hydrochloric acid. Hydrochloric acid is also known as Muriatic acid. Used in industrial applications, swimming pools, and pickle pots used in soldering, this colorless, odorless acid is created when hydrogen chloride mixes with water.

Ferric chloride is used to etch circuit boards and is also known as circuit board solution. In some communities, it is available at Radio Shack or other computer supply outlets. You also can order it online from chemical supply houses. It is actually a salt rather than an acid. When mixed with water, it creates heat and a corrosive action that erodes copper, brass, or thin steel. It has no effect on silver or gold.

Now that you know about the etching chemical you are using, you need to choose what resist to use. Etching is a process with two key variants: the resist you apply at the beginning of the process and the solvent used to dissolve it after the metal has been etched. To make sure you identify the appropriate solvent to remove the resist when you finish etching your metal, refer to the following table.

Etching Resists and Solvents

Resist	Solvent
Permanent marker or stop-out varnish	Rubbing alcohol
Permanent marker, nail polish or duct tape residue	Acetone
Paint	Turpentine

Read though all of the supplies and variants to choose which direction to take your etching project.

To etch metal following the steps in this chapter, you need these supplies:

- Copper or brass
- Wet/dry sandpaper or green scrubbing pad
- Water
- Tape (packing, duct, or electrical)
- Resist, with appropriate solvent
- Three containers, nonmetal
- Ferric chloride
- Ammonia
- Clock or timer
- Toothpicks
- Towel or cotton balls

> **SAFE 'SMITHING**
>
> Asphaltum is a traditional resist that has been used in etching for years. The solvent for asphaltum is naptha, which is an extremely volatile chemical. It can explode if exposed to high temperatures. I don't recommend it in a beginner's home studio without an excellent system of ventilation, a properly rated respirator, and a locking chemical storage cabinet placed outside living areas. Other methods of removing asphaltum are laborious or dangerous as well.

After you gather your supplies, prepare your metal to accept the etchant. Roughing up one side of your metal will help it to more readily accept the etchant. Using either a green scrubbing pad or some wet/dry sandpaper and a little water, scrub the surface of the metal on one side. (Bon Ami cleanser mixed with a little water also removes oils and cleans metal to prepare it for etching.) Rinse your metal with water. When water runs off the metal in sheets, it is clean. If water beads up on the metal, it is not clean. Once your metal is clean and prepared, handle it only by the edges.

Next, create your design by applying your choice of resists. Here are three options:

- **Drawing.** Draw a design directly on your metal with a permanent marker, paint, nail polish, or stop-out varnish.

- **Scratching.** Cover the entire surface of the metal with permanent marker, paint, or stop-out varnish. Once the surface is dry, scratch through the resist to reveal bare metal.

- **Stenciling.** Create a stencil of your own design. Use duct tape to cut it out with scissors or a utility knife. Apply it to clean metal and smooth it well.

After you have applied your design to the front of the metal, protect the back and sides of the metal from the etchant. "Paint" the sides with a permanent marker. Cover the back with a piece of packing or duct tape. I like to fashion a long tab out of the tape, and double it over. This way, I can easily find and pick up the metal from the chemical bath to check etching progress.

You can draw a design for metal etching by using permanent marker as a resist.

Etching Copper and Brass with Ferric Chloride

Once you have applied your design, you are ready to etch. Prepare for safety by wearing gloves, goggles, a respirator, and an apron. Turn on your ventilation. Then follow these steps:

Pour ferric chloride into water to make an etchant bath.

1. Prepare etchant bath. Add about ½ inch of water (1.25 centimeters) into the first of three nonmetal containers. Then slowly pour about a half-inch of ferric chloride into the same container.

2. Prepare rinse bath by adding 2 inches (5 centimeters) of water to the second container. You can use the same container of rinse water throughout your etching session.

3. Prepare neutralization bath in the third container. Open the lid of the ammonia bottle away from your face. Pour about 1 inch (2.5 centimeters) of ammonia into the container.

Place your metal into the etchant bath using the tape tab you made. You can also add a long piece of packing tape to the tab on the back. Fold the ends of the long pieces over either side of the etchant container, suspending the work in the etchant. This setup allows precipitants to fall to the bottom of the etchant container. Either way, you'll want to lift the work out of the etchant every 5 to 10 minutes to release any trapped air bubbles. The total amount of time to leave the work in the bath varies. With a fresh batch of etchant, set a timer for 20 minutes. When the timer sounds, make sure your gear is still on.

Follow these steps to complete the etching process:

1. Check your etch. Pick up your metal using the tape tab. Rinse it briefly in the rinse bath. Use a toothpick to check the depth of your etch.

2. If the etch isn't deep enough, place it back into the etchant bath and set your timer for another 20 minutes. Continue the rinse and check step until you feel satisfied that the etching is deep enough. This process can be as long as 2 hours.

Check the etching every 20 minutes until it is the depth you want.

Acetone is rubbed on etched metal to remove the permanent marker resist.

3. Once the metal is etched to your delight, neutralize the ferric chloride by placing your metal in the ammonia for a minute.

4. Rinse the metal well with fresh water.

5. Apply the appropriate solvent to your metal and rub it with the edge of a towel or some cotton balls. The tape tab comes in handy to hold metal steady during this process.

6. When the metal is clean, gently peel the tape away from the back side and remove the tape tab. If sticky residue remains, use acetone or nail polish remover to take it off.

Now you have completed an etched piece of metal. Enjoy creating jewelry using metal etched with your own imagination. To further enhance the visual depth of your etched surface, consider using an applied patina (see Chapter 10).

This metal has an etched texture.

Photo Etching

You can do another type of etching using ferric chloride. It's a low-tech photo etching process. In this process, an image printed onto special paper is ironed onto clean copper or brass. When the paper is peeled away, a resist in the form of the image is left behind. Then the etching follows the process outlined previously.

You need the specialty paper, known as Press-n-Peel, or PnP, or blue PnP. The paper is blue in color and is sometimes sold in single sheets. It's also available in packets containing multiple sheets. It can cost around $5 per sheet.

You must use a laser printer or a large-capacity copy machine to copy the image to the paper. Inkjet printers and desktop copiers will not work. Then you cut out the image and apply it to clean metal. Press a warm iron on the metal for a few minutes, occasionally checking to see whether the image has adhered to the metal. Usually you can see the paper turn dark as the ink settles and melts to the surface of the metal. Allow the metal to cool. Slowly peel the paper from the metal. If any areas have not transferred, fill them in with a permanent marker. Proceed with the same steps for etching your own image in the previous section.

> **SAFE 'SMITHING**
>
> If you want to etch on silver, the procedures are the same as for etching on brass or copper, except ferric chloride will not work. You must use nitric acid. It must be mixed in a 1:3 ratio with water. It's quite caustic, and the fumes can quickly irritate your lungs. If splashed on skin, it burns on contact. It's also quite expensive. If you do decide to use this chemical, make absolutely sure you have all safety precautions in place including excellent ventilation, protective gear, and a respirator rated for fumes.

Other Texture Options

There are more surface design options than I have room to write about in the pages of this book. In this section, you get a brief overview of some techniques and tools to expand your ideas for creating texture on metal.

Chasing and Repoussé

Chasing is working a design onto the front of metal using gentle, measured force to displace the material, creating the desired imagery. This technique results in textures and the creation of receding areas. Repoussé is working a design onto metal from the back in a similar way, creating volume by pushing metal outward from behind. These ancient techniques are often used together. A series of specific punches, similar to stamping tools, are used to create dimensional designs. A pitch pot with warm pitch is used to grip the metal in place. The placement of the tool and the tap of the hammer occur thousands of times to create even a small-scale design. The beauty and dimensionality of this technique cannot be denied. Nancy Megan Corwin skillfully addresses this branch of metalsmithing in her excellent book *Chasing and Repoussé: Methods Ancient and Modern*.

A Rolling Mill

A rolling mill serves to take thick gauges of metal and wire and thin them down. Another benefit of the rolling mill is that its precision rollers can create texture on metal. All you need to do is make a sandwich.

Use a piece of annealed metal, a piece of heavy paper or manila file folder twice the width of your metal, and a texture maker. Fold the heavy paper to create a small folder. Place the annealed metal inside, making sure there is a small border of paper left around the metal. Then place a textural item on top of the metal and close the packet. This is your sandwich. You can also use two small sheets of brass to make your sandwich. It provides a safe way to use sturdier materials, such as steel wire or screening, that might poke through manila folder material and damage rollers.

You can use hundreds of different things in the sandwich. A few ideas are lace, paper doilies, woven fabric, vegetable bags, paper towel, brown paper bag, screen door fabric, string, thin wire shapes, and dried organic materials. Anything with a definite texture works. What doesn't work well is anything wet or harder than the steel of the rollers in the mill. You do not want to damage this equipment by placing something into your sandwich that would damage the rollers or cause rust.

Open the jaws of rollers just enough to accept the sandwich. Tighten the rollers down about half a turn. Use the big arm and make a smooth rotation. Turn the packet around and repeat the rolling action. Remove the metal from the packet. If you want to continue, anneal the metal again before making more passes through the mill.

A Car

If you don't own a rolling mill and if you have access to a car, you can still try a high-pressure technique. Place your annealed metal under the tire of your car and slowly drive back and forth over it a few times. You're going to see some pretty radical texture. Plus you can tell your friends that you used a two-ton press on your metal.

No car? Place your annealed metal on a cinder block, brick, or concrete floor. Hammer your metal with a rawhide mallet or dance on it and experience another way to create texture. Use your imagination and sense of adventure to search for your own spin on surface design.

CHAPTER 10

Coloring Your Metal

In This Chapter

- The beauty of patinas
- Fuming and direct-contact patinas with ammonia
- Liver of sulfur and peanut oil patinas
- Colored pencil, alcohol ink, and other options

The ability to create color on metal opens up new worlds in jewelry making. Seeing the vibrant, misty, or moody effects of color on metal jewelry can be awe-inspiring. You can get there, too, with some step-by-step guidance and an attitude of adventure!

When color is applied to metal, it is called a *patina*. Patinas are achieved by metals reacting to chemicals in ways that are unfamiliar to most people. The quantities and formulations are staggering, and it's easy to become overwhelmed by the possibilities. The results can be fleeting, too. A patina is a living thing, and it will change over time.

This chapter defines patinas and narrows down a wide field of competitors to a few tried-and-true winners. I explain which patinas are most approachable, how you can use them to safely produce beautiful results, and how to protect the finish. Having a good grasp of just a few of these metal-coloring options will satisfy your craving for color for a long time.

Patina from a Metalsmith's Perspective

The typical dictionary definition of patina is usually a green color on copper or bronze that has either developed over a long period of time (like on a copper roof) or been achieved with acids. Patina also refers to the surface of something that has grown beautiful through wear.

In a metalsmith's world, however, the word *patina* means so much more. For years, metalsmiths the world over have attempted to create all kinds of colors on metal. These days, every color of the rainbow is possible with the right choice of chemicals, oxides, acids, coatings, heat, or varying combinations of these. In this book, I refer to all surface coloring collectively as patinas (except for enamels, which I also discuss later in this chapter).

A high-shine, mirror finish can be beautiful, but my heart longs for the warmth and depth only an applied patina can provide. There is something special about the coloration of metal that lends it a certain beauty. When that coloration mimics the look of the ages, as though that work had been around and loved for a long time, that's something pretty special.

Besides lending metal a beloved, bespoke look, a patina can also be used in more modern ways. Properly prepared, metal can be made to say so many things. From simple spray paint to colored pencil to the complex anodizing of metal using harsh chemicals and electrodes similar to Frankenstein's lab, much can be done to bring a sleek, modern, surprising look to metal. Ancient or modern, there's a patina for that.

A properly applied patina on a finished piece of jewelry can take a design from Saturday afternoon craft to wearable art. When you tell someone you made the earrings you're wearing, wouldn't you rather hear a "Wow!" than an obligatory "Nice"?

In this chapter, I show you some pieces of jewelry pre- and post-patina application. It will be easy to see the difference, and I hope it'll inspire you to see what you can make in your own jewelry laboratory—no evil scientist needed!

This "Soji" fabricated, etched sterling silver pendant has a liver of sulfur patina.

> **ARTISAN TIP**
>
> Patinas are typically applied as the last step in jewelry making. An exception may occur if you want to set a delicate gemstone or pearl that should not come into contact with heat or chemical patinas. Apply the patina to finished jewelry and then set the stone or epoxy the pearl on a cleaned-up area of metal, taking care not to scratch or scrape the delicate patina surface. No patina will cover gouges or sloppy soldering, so prepare accordingly.

Low-Tech Patinas from Household Items

You can apply patinas to your finished jewelry with a few ingredients you probably already have around your home, such as ammonia, table salt, and peanut oil. With some minor preparation, important safety precautions, and finishing techniques, you'll be creating lovely patinas in no time.

The color of patina you achieve depends on the type of metal you used and how you prepare it, how the patina is prepared and applied, and what steps are taken to preserve the finish. As with all patinas, these colorations are applied as a last step in the jewelry-making process. After you have applied your chosen patina, use fine-grit sandpaper, fine steel wool, or a piece of denim to reveal some original metal and create interesting high-low effects. Seal your patina with an applied wax, such as Renaissance Wax or Johnson's Paste Wax, or an acrylic spray finish.

Preparing Metal for a Patina

To prepare metal for patina application, clean it with water and a good degreasing detergent, such as Dawn dishwashing liquid, and a soft toothbrush or brass brush or 500-grit wet/dry sandpaper. When water sheets off the metal, it is clean. If the water beads up on the metal, it is not clean. When the metal is clean, avoid touching it. Instead, use tweezers or hold pieces by the edges to transport it from place to place.

Brass resists patinas until it is copper-plated. To deposit a layer of copper onto a brass or Nu-Gold surface, grab some warm pickle solution (used for the removal of oxides that occur on metal after heating with a torch) from your pickle pot and place it in a separate glass or ceramic container. The process works best with deep blue pickle, which is saturated with lots of copper oxides. Place the metal in the container of pickle solution. Using tweezers wrapped in a bit of steel wool, swab the item to be plated. This creates an electrostatic plating action. Any metal that the steel wool touches will become copper-plated, including stainless steel tools, silver solder, and sterling silver. In fact, this plating method works beautifully to copper-plate any unwanted areas of silver solder on copper pieces. Your soldered copper jewelry will then have a uniform finished look.

Copper plating on brass takes place as steel wool contacts the brass. The jar contains warm pickle solution.

Creating Home-Brew Patinas

You can easily apply your first home-brew patina, ammonia, to produce a blue-green color on copper. As with many patinas, there's more than one way to get the coloration, namely, *fuming* and direct contact.

> **DEFINITION**
>
> **Fuming** is an atmospheric method of applying a patina to metal. In other words, vapors do the work of changing the color of the metal.

The method you use for the first experiment is fuming. If you've seen copper drains, roof flashing, and statuary that's turned green, this change is caused by a natural fuming process. This process can be re-created in the studio in the controlled environment of a bucket. In the direct contact method, the patina solution, ammonia in this case, contacts the metal directly through the application of sawdust, kitty litter, dry rice, dry leaves, or corn cob meal.

These methods won't work on silver or gold. With some special preparation, they can be made to work on brass if the metal has been plated with copper. (See the preceding section for how to copper-plate brass to prepare it for an ammonia patina.)

> **SAFE 'SMITHING**
>
> When using ammonia, be aware that the fumes have a strong, caustic odor and can be aggressive on eyes, skin, and mucous membranes. Be prepared with ventilation, gloves, goggles, and a respirator as needed. If you cannot tolerate ammonia or want a less-caustic option, try substituting white vinegar for a slightly different result.

To begin, you need some supplies. Obviously you need your prepared jewelry. You also need the following:

- Fan or ventilation
- Gloves
- Goggles
- Plastic bucket

- Glass or plastic dish
- Covering for bucket, such as a plastic bag
- Ammonia, nonsudsy
- Water

Optional items:

- Wire
- Tape, any kind
- Salt, any kind
- White vinegar

- Sandpaper in various grits
- Wax or spray varnish
- Soft-bristled brush

Creating a Fumed Ammonia Patina

Wearing the gloves and goggles, and with the ventilation going, you can create a fumed ammonia patina. Here's what to do:

1. Pour enough ammonia to cover the bottom of the bucket by about ½ inch (1.25 centimeters).

2. Wet your jewelry item, either with the water or ammonia, or use the optional white vinegar. You can do this by brushing or dipping the jewelry.

3. Turn the dish upside down and place the jewelry on top of it so that it is sitting above the ammonia. Or suspend the jewelry from wire above the ammonia. If you are applying patina to more that one item, be sure items aren't nested too closely together or the patina won't develop evenly.

4. Cover the bucket with a plastic bag, and wait for the desired color to develop. It takes a few hours or overnight for a blue-green patina to fully develop. To check progress, open the bucket's covering away from your face.

5. When the piece is the color you like, remove the jewelry, rinse it very gently and allow it to dry.

6. Use a soft bristle brush to gently remove flaking or excess patina. As the metal dries, color will continue to develop.

7. Seal the jewelry as you like with either a wax or spray varnish to protect the patina. A coat of spray varnish will stabilize the patina before you sand it, and then again when you are done with all sanding and finishing operations.

A white plastic juice can turned upside down holds clean, damp copper ready for fuming. The blue bucket contains ammonia.

The bucket procedure may be repeated, with brushing or scrubbing between layers to build up a different variety of patina effects. These few more tips will help you in your patina adventure:

- Dampening jewelry first helps the patina formation process; dry metal won't receive color.

- Sprinkle a little salt on clean, wet metal for a different effect. The patina grows crusty around the grains of salt.

- Ammonia becomes inert, or "spent," over time and no longer has an effect on metal. If you don't detect an odor to the ammonia, the patina won't develop.

- A warm environment speeds the patina process.

- I recommend a spray matte varnish sealer on this patina. A wax finish tends to overly disturb and darken this delicate patina.

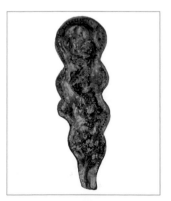

This blue patina is the result of 10 hours inside the bucket.

This completed piece has been sealed once and then sanded and sealed again using matte spray varnish.

Creating a Direct-Contact Ammonia Patina

With the direct contact method, you can use sawdust or clean kitty litter (any variety) to apply the ammonia directly to the metal. Each material produces different effects.

Follow these steps:

1. Place enough of your selected material (sawdust, litter, and so on) to cover your jewelry in a resealable plastic bag.

2. Saturate the material with ammonia, draining off any excess liquid.

3. Sprinkle in some salt, close the bag, and knead the bag to distribute the ingredients.

4. Open the bag, place your clean jewelry inside, and close the bag.

5. Place the bag in a sunny or warm area and leave it alone for a few hours, overnight, or longer. Shifting the contents of the bag may disturb the development of the patina. Wait for your desired color to develop.

6. When the patina is the color you want, remove your jewelry and allow it to dry.

7. Gently rinse or brush your jewelry to remove excess dried material.

The type of wood the sawdust came from and the size of the sawdust particles will have an effect on the patina. Play around with different types to get different results. Try other absorbent materials, such as fresh or dried leaves, string, or shredded fabric.

This copper and sterling pendant is ready for the direct-contact ammonia, sawdust, and salt patina.

The copper and sterling pendant has just been removed from the direct-contact ammonia, sawdust, and salt patina.

Creating a Peanut Oil Patina

Peanut oil offers a simple, richly colored, and surprisingly tough patina to many metal surfaces free of gemstones. About the only thing you need to worry about is a peanut allergy. If you are allergic, skip this option. This patina also requires the use of heat. Take care not to use heat on pearls or heat-sensitive gemstones.

Follow these steps:

1. Brush peanut oil on clean metal, and wipe away excess oil until only a thin layer remains.

2. Warm the metal gently and slowly with a soft torch flame (use the flickering tail of the flame rather than the hot blue area). A small crème brûlée torch will work.

3. When the peanut oil begins to smoke, remove the flame and allow the piece to cool. If the work remains sticky after cooling, try reheating again very gently.

This copper is being gently tickled with the torch flame.

This copper leaf pendant shows that a peanut oil finish can be both beautiful and variable.

You can also use a toaster oven or conventional oven with peanut oil to achieve more evenly controlled results:

1. Place the clean item on a tray or baking sheet and place inside a 300 degrees Fahrenheit (149 degrees Celsius) oven.

2. Observe the piece every few minutes until you like the color development.

3. Carefully remove the tray. Not only will the work be hot, it also will be sticky until it cools. Any touch will remove the patina you just created. Allow the item to cool undisturbed.

You don't need to do anything else to this tough patina, unless you wish to remove some of it from high points using 400-grit wet/dry sandpaper, used dry, to reveal the brighter metal underneath.

Next-Step-Up Chemical Patinas

For a chemical patina, concentrate on a single, incredibly versatile ingredient known as *liver of sulfur*, or LOS. I call LOS the king of patinas because you can do so much with it. When you apply it to silver, copper, and brass, you can achieve colors from black to shades of browns, blues, and pinks with iridescent undertones.

> **DEFINITION**
>
> **Liver of sulfur** (LOS) is potassium sulfide, typically found in lump form. It creates a patina when it is dissolved in water and applied to sterling silver and copper. It also can be found in an extended-life gel. Buying it in liquid form isn't recommended, as the shelf life is very short.

Liver of sulfur also has a distinctive, inescapable rotten-egg odor. Be sure to work in a well-ventilated area or outdoors. Don't let the stink keep you from trying out this magnificent patina, though.

Preparing Your Jewelry and Gathering Supplies

Jewelry preparation is important because the metal must be completely grease-free. Clean surfaces with tap water and a good degreasing detergent, like Dawn dishwashing liquid, using a soft toothbrush or brass brush or 500-grit wet/dry sandpaper. Do not use steel wool as it contains oils.

Once the metal is clean, avoid touching it. Instead, use tweezers or hold the jewelry by the edges to transport it from place to place. With your squeaky-clean jewelry standing by, you're ready for some fun. Here's what else you need:

- Fan or ventilation
- Newspaper or paper towels
- Gloves
- Goggles
- Glass jar with lid (for patina)

- Two plastic containers (about 2 cups/500 milliliters) with tap water
- Baking soda
- Tongs or tweezers
- Heat source (a hot plate or hot water)
- Liver of sulfur, pea-sized lump

Optional:

- Distilled water
- A length of thin wire formed into a hook
- Saucepan

I like to set up my workstation, protected with paper towels or newspaper, with the patina on the left; plain water for rinsing in the middle; and a container with water and 3 tablespoons (45 milliliters) of baking soda for neutralizing, also known as a *stop bath*, on the right.

Cooking the Patina

Cook up the patina by following these steps:

1. Using tongs or tweezers, place a pea-sized lump of liver of sulfur into the jar of warm tap or distilled water.

2. Replace the lid and return your container of LOS to its storage place immediately.

3. If using a hot plate, place the jar containing the patina in a 1-inch (2.50 centimeters) deep bath of tap water in a saucepan.

4. Place the saucepan on warm hot plate. Otherwise, simply use hot tap water.

5. Stir the water to dissolve the lump of LOS. It should be a clear lemon-yellow color, and, of course, it will stink.

These clean, textured copper earring dangles, back-to-back on a wire hook, are ready for a liver of sulfur bath.

The same earring dangles after about 8 to 10 dip-rinse-dip cycles in the liver of sulfur bath.

Coloring Then Neutralizing

Dip your jewelry into the LOS solution using tongs or a piece of hooked wire. Then dip it into the plain water. Continue to dip and check, watching the progression of colors. Stop when the color pleases you and immerse in the neutralizing bath of baking soda and water. Allow the jewelry to dry.

To help contain odors, put a lid on the LOS solution in between dipping activities. When the solution becomes clear, it is no longer effective. Discard it according to package directions. Room temperature LOS that has maintained a clear yellow color will still work to patina your jewelry, but it will be slow. To speed up the effect, run jewelry under hot water to warm it up, and then dip it in the LOS. Repeat this process until the desired color is reached.

Don't immerse jewelry with soft gems like pearls or delicate embellishments into the hot patina. Instead, gently warm your jewelry in a plain hot water bath and use a small artist's brush to paint on LOS instead. Continue until you're happy with the patina and then neutralize with a baking soda and water mixture and allow it to dry.

Finishing

I consider a liver of sulfur patina to be permanent. When properly applied, this patina won't flake or rub off. It does not come off in a pickle pot. Permanent, however, is a relative term. Some or most of the patina can be removed with light sanding to create attractive, bright high points to contrast with darker areas in recesses.

To seal in your patina for a long period of time, wax it or spray it with an acrylic sealer. These methods will slightly alter the look of your patina. Chapter 13 has more information on these methods. As with all aspects of jewelry making, careful experimentation and a little bit of experience will leave you with jewelry fit for royalty!

These copper earring dangles were added to ear wires and treated with a liver of sulfur patina, and then embellished with freshwater pearls.

METAL MISHAP

A liver of sulfur patina can be removed only by burning it off with a torch flame (if no gemstones are present) or wiping it with Tarn-X (active ingredient: sulfamic acid), a strong, tarnish-removing product available at many hardware stores. Ventilation is needed with these methods.

Metals left to right: copper, sterling silver, nickel silver, Nu-Gold (brass alloy), and copper-plated Nu-Gold await patina.

After the patina process, the surface of each test piece has been lightly dry sanded in selected areas with 500-grit wet/dry sandpaper.

Overview of Other Techniques

There are boatloads of other interesting patinas you can use on metal. A few approachable ones are described in the following sections. These methods work best on sterling silver, copper, and brass, or Nu-Gold. Remember that, as with all patinas, your results will depend on what type of metal you use, how you prepare it, how you apply the patina, and how you finish and seal the work. When you are ready for more patina challenges, any of these methods can be a lot of fun.

Colored Pencil

Colored pencil is a newer method of achieving color on metal, and you can achieve some stunning, painterly effects. This method works best when it is applied to a foundation of metal that has been primed with a liver of sulfur patina. Using higher-quality pencils built up in thin layers with a coat of mineral spirits brushed between layers seems to work well. The final layer is then sealed with a few very light layers of clear acrylic sealer, in either a glossy or matte finish. All soldering, filing, and sanding should be completed before applying colored pencil treatments to metal. Many secrets still await discovery by the clever jewelry maker who tackles this elusive technique.

Alcohol Inks

Experiments with alcohol inks on metal produce some exciting, deeply colorful results. This is another method that seems to work best with a "background" of liver of sulfur patina applied first. Try removing some of the liver of sulfur patina with 500-grit wet/dry sandpaper before applying the ink in one area at a time.

Keep in mind that these inks don't overlap well. They can be dripped on one color at a time straight from the bottle, blended together and applied, or diluted with a special solvent sold with the alcohol inks and used when you want a softer effect. Inks are sticky until they dry to a slightly glossy finish. Seal with a clear matte or gloss acrylic spray applied in a few quick, light coats. Don't apply a wax sealer because it will take the color right back off.

A drawback to this technique is that the color fades over time and is delicate. It is best used on jewelry pieces that receive lower-impact wear, such as pendants and earrings, rather than rings or bracelets. Consider reapplying any fading ink after a few years.

> **SAFE 'SMITHING**
>
> Beware of fumes and particulates. Be sure to use spray paints and solvents in a well-ventilated area and use a respirator as needed. Use a dust mask whenever sanding creates airborne particles. Follow all safety precautions on product labels.

Heat Patina

You can use a torch flame to create a patina on metal. This method works on your finished jewelry or metal components that you can use in the jewelry-making process. Don't use this method on any gemstone unless you are 100 percent certain it can take the heat.

With your torch lit, move the feathery end of the flame over the surface of your metal, and stop when the color pleases you. On copper, try heating metal to brilliant orange, and then immediately quenching it in cold water for a permanent orange-red color. If you are not happy with your results, place your item in a warm pickle for five minutes, neutralize it in a baking soda and water bath, dry it, and repeat the experiment.

Enameling

Enameling is the art of fusing powdered glass to a surface. Enamels are available in many translucent and opaque colors, in lead-bearing and non–lead-bearing varieties. Enameling can be done on copper, steel, fine silver, or gold.

Enamellists spend careers working in the field and entire books and courses of study are devoted to the art of enameling. If the idea of this type of effect intrigues you, by all means investigate it further. Even a few different colors of powdered enamel on your jewelry can offer some lovely results.

Willa's Journey pendant is enameled, fabricated, textured, sewn, and patinated and contains a raw emerald.

Adding Gems and Embellishments

In This Chapter

- Top ten gems for beginners
- Bargain gems and basic settings
- Two settings from scratch: one with soldering and one without
- A method for securing found objects

The preciousness of gemstones changes with the ages. Syndicates attempt to control our notions of preciousness for a common stone—the diamond. Fashion mavens dictate favorite colors with each passing season. That's a preciousness based on trend. Cultures heavily identify with certain gemstone varieties, imbuing them with their own value. Man has even waged war over gemstones.

It's kind of hard to get a grip on gemstones with all of the emotionally charged history around them! This chapter cuts through the clutter by lasering in on a handful of reasonably priced gemstones. You can try these varieties in your beginning metal projects, using them as accents or centerpieces for your jewelry designs.

This chapter starts you off on your jewelry destiny with how-tos on creating basic settings, including lots of tips and tricks. There is even some information on using found objects in your work. By the end of this chapter, you may find a new way to define preciousness.

Buying Gems

Early on in my metalsmithing pursuits, my first instructor, Marilyn Smith, rocked my world with a simple errand. She sent me to the local rock hound to shop for a gemstone. I was to spend no more than $5. Thinking that must be a mistake, I went to the location. I asked if there were any stones for $5 or less. As trays of stones were laid before me, something changed inside me. I didn't have to pay a lot for a beautiful gemstone. And you don't either!

This pair of earrings feature a red jasper gemstone in a silver setting.

(© Paul D'Andrea)

Gemstone Characteristics

When shopping for a gemstone, you'll have many choices. First among them is how they're cut. The two key types of cuts are *faceted* stones and *cabochons*. A cross between the two is called *rose cut*, which features triangular facets on the top and a smooth bottom. The primary focus in this chapter is on traditional faceted and cabochon gemstones.

Faceted stones may be cut by hand or machine and may be natural or man-made. Faceted stones are available in many price ranges. I've paid less than a dollar for some small, faceted man-made stones.

Cabochons are typically offered as smooth-top stones, with smooth sides and a flat bottom. However, the surface can vary. Some gemstone surfaces, such as drusy quartz, are rough and jagged. You'll also run across cabochon stones with flat tops, called *buff tops*, as well as cabochons with flat planes cut at irregular angles. To facilitate setting, your cabochon must have a flat back. A poorly cut cabochon can rock around inside the setting, giving you fits when trying to set it. The stone can also break under the incredible pressure needed to bend metal over it. The most common cabochon shapes are round and oval. Freeform cabochons are available in organic, nonuniform shapes. These gemstones are also available in every conceivable price range. They aren't inherently less expensive than faceted gems.

> **DEFINITION**
>
> **Faceted** stones have been cut into facets, or planes, that reflect light. **Cabochons** are stones that have not been cut into facets.

An assortment of six oval cabochon gems.

Color is another important consideration when choosing stones for your jewelry. Note that color is likely to be a bit uneven in natural stones. Only man-made stones are perfect in color.

In addition to being classified by cut and color, gems have a certain degree of hardness. There are several scales of measuring this characteristic. One of the more well-known is called the Mohs Scale of Hardness for minerals. The scale denotes the number 1 for the softest mineral and 10 for the hardest. A diamond is an example of a stone classified as 10 in hardness.

How hard a stone is will dictate, to a degree, how it's set. A gemstone of 6 or less on the Mohs Scale of Hardness is best set with lots of metal around it to protect it. Softer gems can be safely used in earrings and necklaces that receive less wear. Rings receive a lot of abuse, so harder stones are best used in them. Appendix B has more information about the Mohs Scale of Hardness.

A gemstone's rarity, cut, color, hardness, artificial treatment, shipping costs, middleman markup, and public demand all play a role in the price you will pay for a gemstone. When choosing any gem, look for polished edges and no fractures. And always keep in mind the setting you'll use when you get those pretty things home. If you can't fabricate the setting for that stone, you may want to pass it by for something you can have more success with.

Shop for These Stones First

To help you cut through lots of gemstone options fast, review the following table. It has my top 10 gemstone picks for beginners. Some of the stones are available in both cabochon and faceted styles, which is listed in the Comments column, along with color information.

You can find most of these gemstones for low prices, depending on the size, quality, and quantity you buy. Your location will make a difference in price and availability.

Top 10 Gemstone Picks for Beginners

Name	Mohs Hardness	Comments
Agate	7	Many colors, cabochons
Amethyst	7	Purple, cabochons and faceted
Carnelian	7	Rich orange red, cabochons
Garnet	7	Reds to plums, cabochons and faceted
Jasper	7	Many colors, cabochons
Onyx	7	Many colors, cabochons
Pearl	3	Many colors and shapes
Quartz	7	Many colors, cabochons and faceted
Sapphire	9	All colors including white, cabochons and faceted
Turquoise	6	Blues and greens, cabochons

> **ARTISAN TIP**
>
> Most dealers will give you a break if you buy more than one of the same stone. In fact, I recommend you purchase at least two of the same stone when you buy stones. Because you never know what could happen during stone setting. If one breaks or gets lost, you can grab for the backup stone instead of going for the box of tissues.

Most dealers are very helpful with beginning gem buyers. Their business is built on their good reputation, and they want to keep it intact. They also want to keep you coming back for more gems. So don't be afraid to ask them questions.

Setting Gems

The care you take in the objects you set will elevate them to heights they could not achieve alone. Cost is not a factor. Gemstones, like the Velveteen Rabbit of childhood lore, come to life when they're loved. They glow when they're worn. They're cared for, admired, and passed along to family. They can last for generations.

To learn more about the ways gemstones are set and some ground-floor basics on setting your own gems, read on.

Basic Gemstone Settings

Gemstones are set in several ways. The basic settings include bezel, tube, prong, and peg. Advanced stone setting types include crown, gypsy, or flush mounts; these are for faceted gemstones.

In a *bezel* setting, a thin band of metal known as *bezel wire* is soldered to a back plate. This creates a setting called a *bezel cup*. The stone fits inside the bezel cup and rests on the back plate. The bezel wire is pushed over the stone and smoothed firmly. This setting is most often used to set cabochon stones, and is usually made from fine silver wire, but not always. Bezel wire may be purchased in varying band widths, or you may cut your own band from thin metal. Bezel cups may be purchased premade in standard sizes.

In a *tube* setting, a length of silver tubing is cut to fit the height of a faceted stone. The tube is soldered to the body of the jewelry item. Then a seat is cut inside the tubing to accommodate the stone. The stone is set with specialty stone-setting tools. Tube settings may be purchased in standard sizes.

In a *prong* setting, wires are arranged in a pattern that will wrap the gemstone. The arrangement is soldered together, and the prongs are trimmed and refined to fit the gemstone. The prongs are then pushed over the stone to secure it. Prong settings can be used for faceted or cabochon stones. The Chapter 14 project called Captured Canyon features a prong setting.

A *peg* setting is also known as pearl setting. A wire that fits snugly into a half-drilled pearl or other object is soldered to a back plate or cup. The peg is scribed with lines or file marks to create a place for epoxy to anchor itself. A drop of epoxy is placed on the peg, and then the pearl or object is attached.

This silver necklace has a tube-set faceted gem and a freeform turquoise cabochon.

The gold pearls in this pair of silver earrings are set with pegs.

(© Paul D'Andrea)

The first setting most metalsmiths learn how to make is a bezel setting for cabochon stones. In the following sections, I tell you how to make two versions. One version is a fabricated bezel cup, which you'll cut to fit your stone and use soldering to complete. The other is a solder-free way to capture a cabochon.

Basic Soldered Setting

A soldered bezel setting for cabochons is a great lesson in fabrication and fitting skills for any metalsmith. Be sure to allow an afternoon to fabricate your bezel setting, so you won't feel rushed to completion.

> **ARTISAN TIP**
>
> For your first project, consider choosing a round or oval cabochon that's at least ¼ inch (.75 centimeter) but no more than 1 inch (2.5 centimeters) in diameter. You'll be able to solder and fabricate more easily with those sizes, and you can use a butane micro-torch on settings 1 inch in diameter or less.

To create a basic soldered bezel setting, you need these tools and materials:

- Cabochon
- Sterling silver sheet for back plate, 24 or 22 works fine
- Fine silver bezel wire
- Ultra fine-point permanent marker
- Jeweler's saw with 3/0 saw blades
- Fine-point scissors
- Flat-nose and round-nose pliers
- Number 2 cut hand file
- Half-round needle file
- Bezel pusher
- Scribe
- Burnishing tool
- Torch setup
- Flame-resistant surface
- Pickle and pickle pot
- Copper tongs
- Soldering pick
- Fine-point tweezers
- Silver solders in easy, medium, and hard
- 320-grit wet/dry sandpaper
- Post-it notes
- Double-stick tape
- Bench pin clamped to work surface
- Wooden or steel dowel rod, smaller than diameter of gem
- Dental floss

When you select bezel wire, keep in mind that the height of your bezel wire should measure about one-third of the total height of your gemstone. However, you can use a taller bezel wire, if that's the only wire you have. Simply sand it down after you make the bezel cup.

To create a basic soldered bezel setting, you first need to fit the bezel wire:

1. Place a small piece of double-stick tape on your work surface, and place the gemstone on top of it, pressing down lightly.

2. Cut off the sticky strip on a Post-it note. Wrap it around the gemstone firmly, and mark the point where the paper overlaps.

3. Stick the paper on your bezel wire as a cutting pattern. Use your scissors to cut the bezel wire at this point.

4. Check the fit by wrapping the bezel wire around the gemstone. It must meet all the way up and down the cut ends of the bezel wire. Refine with scissors or with your flat file to make a good fit.

Use a strip of paper to measure the circumference of a round cabochon to figure out the right length for the bezel wire.

A small solder chip rests on a silver bezel wire seam, ready to be heated.

This silver bezel fits this purple gem well.

The next step is to solder the bezel closed:

1. Grip the bezel wire in the jaws of flat-nose pliers to line up the seam. Your bezel wire will be flattened, rather than round, after you do this. Set the pliers aside, and hold each end of the bezel wire between thumb and forefinger. Use a bit of back-and-forth movement to create tension to hold the bezel closed.

2. Apply flux to the bezel seam, inside and out.

3. Place a chip of hard solder on the seam, creating a bridge between the two ends. Then place the bezel on your flame-resistant surface.

4. Turn on the torch and heat up the area on either side of the bezel wire until the water in the flux bubbles and burns off. Keep your soldering pick in your dominant hand to make any adjustments to the solder chip. Do not apply high heat directly to the bezel wire. Keeping the heat moving, watch for the flux to become clear, and then for the solder to melt. You'll see a flash of silver when that happens.

5. Quench the bezel in water, pickle for five minutes, neutralize, rinse, and dry.

Check the bezel fit again by placing the bezel over the gemstone. If it's too big, cut the solder out from either side of the seam using scissors, and repeat the fitting and soldering steps. If it's too small, take the dowel rod and drop the bezel over it. Lay the dowel rod on its side and roll it along your work surface to stretch the bezel wire a bit. Stop and check for fit often.

Now it's time to fit the bezel to the back plate:

1. Place a piece of 320-grit sandpaper on your work surface. If your work surface is uneven, set the sandpaper on a bench block. Sand the bottom of the bezel where it will meet the back plate. Use a figure-eight movement to sand the bezel. Sand quickly but lightly.

2. Check the fit of the bezel on your gemstone again. This checking also serves to reshape the bezel wire.

3. Place the bezel cup on the silver sheet to measure the sheet for the back plate. Leave at least $\frac{1}{8}$ inch (3 millimeters) around the border of the bezel cut. You may choose to make the back plate part of your design by using a larger sheet of metal.

4. Cut out the back plate using a jeweler's saw or metal shears, and then flatten it gently using your fingers or a rawhide mallet. Sand the back plate.

5. Place the bezel on the back plate and hold it up to the light to check for gaps under the bezel. If there are gaps, tap the back plate lightly with a mallet to flatten it. Refine the bezel a bit more with the sandpaper method. Check the fit again.

Once you confirm that the bezel and the back plate fit together with no gaps, you need to join these pieces with solder:

1. Brush flux onto the back plate and the bottom of the bezel wire. Place the assembly on a flameproof surface.

2. Using fine-point tweezers, place small chips of medium solder around the outside of the bezel wire, spaced about $\frac{1}{4}$ inch (6.25 millimeters) apart. Prop the chips against the wall of your bezel to create a ladder between the back plate and bezel. Don't push them all the way up against the bezel wall.

3. Heat the area around the bezel cup assembly with your torch flame until the water in the flux bubbles off. Reposition runaway solder chips with your soldering pick. Larger back plates will take longer to heat.

> **METAL MISHAP**
>
> Solder will travel toward heat, so move the flame to the area where solder needs to flow. Don't put the flame right on the bezel wire, or the wire will melt.

4. When the flux clears, move the heat a bit closer to the back plate. Swirl the flame around the outer edges of the back plate, about one second per revolution. Watch for the flux to turn clear. The solder will slump and then flow, flashing silver around the entire base of the bezel.

These soldering chips are propped up on a silver bezel cup that has had small amounts of metal removed from the edge with sharp scissors and files.

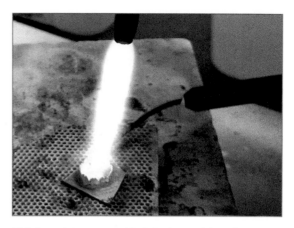

This bezel cup assembly is being soldered.

5. When the solder has flowed, immediately remove the heat. Dribbling a few drops of water onto the hot metal will cool it without warping the back plate.

6. Quench the bezel assembly and pickle it for five minutes.

7. Neutralize the bezel cup, rinse it, and let it dry.

Use dental floss under a gemstone to easily remove it from the setting after you check for fit.

To check the fit of the gemstone again, place a strand of dental floss across your bezel cup. With the floss underneath, nudge the cabochon into the bezel cup to test for fit. Carefully tug on the dental floss to liberate the gemstone from the setting and make any adjustments. If the setting is too tight, use a burnisher or a scribe to slightly stretch the metal. Go around the inside of the bezel cup, pushing outward gently against the wall of the bezel wire.

If the gemstone fits, you have finished with the fabrication. Remove the gem and the dental floss. You can cut away the excess back plate using your jeweler's saw and solder the bezel cup to a larger item using easy solder. If your back plate is part of your design, you can solder items to it now, using easy solder. You can get away with using medium solder if you're careful with torch heat during subsequent soldering operations.

Basic No-Solder Setting

A solder-free setting for cabochons is easy to achieve with a good layout and the careful use of the jeweler's saw. For this setting, you need a round or oval cabochon and some thin metal. Thin metal is much easier to use than thick. A circle or oval template comes in handy when laying out your cutting lines. It's helpful if you start with annealed metal, too. It will make pushing the prongs over a lot easier.

The following tools and materials are needed for a solder-free setting:

- Cabochon
- Sheet metal
- Circles or ovals template to mimic the shape of your gemstone
- Ultra fine-point permanent marker
- Hole-punching pliers, center punch, or drill and small drill bit

- Jeweler's saw with 6/0 saw blades
- Round-nose pliers
- Half-round needle file
- Bezel pusher or toothbrush with the head cut off

Follow these steps to create a solder-free setting:

1. Place your stone on your metal and draw a line around it using the permanent marker.

2. With your template laid over the shape you just drew, find a shape about ⅛ inch (3 millimeters) smaller. Use your ultra fine-point marker to outline that shape directly on your metal, inside the previous shape.

3. Divide your shape into four quadrants, and draw tapering prong locations directly on the metal.

4. Using your marker, fill in the sections of the metal to be cut away. Now you have a pattern for the ledge the gem will rest upon once the prongs are lifted up.

5. Locate a place on the metal that is filled in with marker. Drill a hole there.

6. Cut out around all of the prong points using your jeweler's saw. (I used a 6/0 jeweler's saw blade for the pendant shown in the photos.) Cut down into the ledge along either side of the prong as shown in the photo.

7. From the back side of the metal, use the cut-off toothbrush or bezel pusher to push the prong tips outward.

8. From the front side of the metal, use round-nose pliers to gently pull up the prongs.

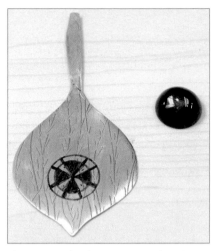

This pre-etched copper pendant is marked for cutting a pattern for a setting to hold a cabochon.

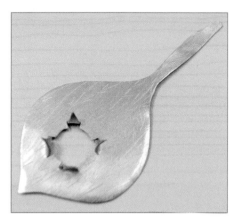

This copper pendant has its prongs lifted and is ready to receive a gemstone.

A copper pendant set with a 10-millimeter onyx gemstone.

9.   Use the needle file to clean up the edges of the prongs as needed.

10.   Test-fit the stone. You may find that you need to cut into the metal with the jeweler's saw a bit more in order to get the stone in there.

11.   Set the stone. Push the prongs over the gemstone and smooth them using the cut-off toothbrush or bezel pusher.

I left a tab of metal at the top of the pendant for a bail. To finish off the pendant, I turned the tab toward the pendant front using round pliers.

Using Found Objects

You can treat found objects just like you would gemstones in your work. You can use either of the previous settings to secure found objects. For example, you can set smooth pebbles and rocks with the solder-free setting. You can set slices of wood in a bezel setting. If the pressure of a bezel wire is too great for a found object to withstand, you can epoxy the found object inside the bezel setting to secure it.

Another option is to solder a peg to your work to hold found objects just as you would a pearl. The technique is the same. You can hold a lot of things this way, such as twigs, small plastic figures, beans, and more.

CHAPTER 12

Making Chains and Other Findings

In This Chapter

- A basic chain
- An easy S-clasp
- A clear-cut coil end cap
- Uncomplicated jump rings
- Effortless ear wires

Findings are the components that make your jewelry wearable. Jump rings are findings that show up everywhere in jewelry making. Even if you purchase them premade, every metalsmith should know how to crank out a few in a pinch. Some findings take center stage, such as chains, clasps, and bails. Others do their work from behind the scenes, such as a pin on the back of a brooch. Handmade ear wires add a distinctive touch to even the simplest earring creation. Get ready to discover several basic, easy ways to elevate your jewelry with findings!

Jump Rings

Jump rings are everywhere in jewelry making! You can certainly purchase all the jump rings you need from any number of terrific suppliers. But you'll want to know how to make your own for those occasions when you need only a few. In this section, I tell you how to make a fistful of jump rings fast.

You can make jump rings in any metal and in any gauge. You can make them in any diameter, dependent only on the size mandrel or dowel rod you have available. Anneal your metal first, if you can. Make sure your metal is clean and dry before beginning.

To make your own jump rings, you need the following supplies:

- Wire in your choice of gauge
- Dowel rod or mandrel the size you want your links
- Jeweler's saw and 3/0 blades
- Bench pin
- Catch tray or cookie sheet
- 320-grit wet/dry sandpaper
- Optional: masking tape

To make jump rings, follow these steps:

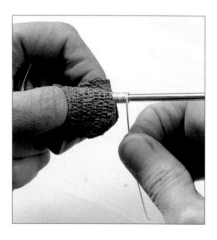

Wrap wire around a mandrel to make jump rings.

1. Wrap the wire around the right-size dowel rod or mandrel for your project, keeping the coils tight and close together. Some metalsmiths prefer to wrap a strip of masking tape around the coil to hold the rings for sawing.

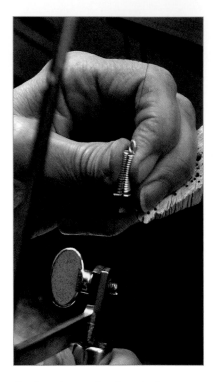

Sawing rings using jeweler's saw.

2. Prop the dowel rod or mandrel against your bench pin for support. Then cut the rings using your jeweler's saw, allowing them to fall into the catch tray or a cookie sheet.

3. Smooth any burs with 320-grit wet/dry sandpaper.

If you have extra jump rings left after finishing your project, store them in small, clear plastic bags and write the gauge wire you used and the dimension of the ring on the bag.

Chains

Chains play an important role in jewelry making. They can serve as a simple, straightforward carrier for a pendant. Or they can be the sole focus of your jewelry project. They can also land in the middle. Whatever role you choose for your chain, keep the overall look in mind as you design your jewelry project. In the end, you'll be rewarded with a complementary relationship between all parts of your work.

Supplies for a Handmade Chain

The fluid, hand-wrought beauty of a crafted chain is a classic point of pride for any metalsmith. If you want to make your own chain, the job starts simply, with jump rings. The number of rings you need depends on the gauge of wire you're using, the size of the rings, and how long you want the finished chain to be. Consider making a short length of chain in your preferred gauge to help you estimate how many links you'll need.

To make your own chain, you need these tools and supplies:

- Annealed sterling silver wire or fine silver wire, which is softer, in your choice of gauge
- Dowel rod or mandrel the size you want your links
- Jeweler's saw and number 3/0 (or finer) blades
- Bench pin
- Catch tray or cookie sheet

- Flat-nose and chain-nose pliers
- Fine-point permanent marker
- Set of needle files
- 400-grit wet/dry sandpaper
- Torch setup (small butane torch will work)
- Pickle pot with pickle solution, neutralizing bath, and plain water bath
- Heatproof surface and flameproof soldering surface
- Hard solder
- Solder pick
- Paste flux
- Flux brush or small artist's brush
- Fine-point tweezers
- Copper tongs
- Clean hand towel or paper towels
- Optional: cross-lock tweezers with insulated grip

> **ARTISAN TIP**
>
> Sterling silver wire is stiffer than fine silver wire. Although you can use either to make the chain, it's best to anneal sterling silver wire before beginning to make the wire easier to coil around a dowel rod or mandrel.

Note that the chain in the project photographs is 18-gauge round sterling silver wire. The rings were wound on a ⅜-inch (1-centimeter) dowel rod and were cut using a 6/0 saw blade in the jeweler's saw.

Steps for Making a Simple Chain

To make a chain, follow these steps:

1. Cut the jump rings by following the previous steps in the "Jump Rings" section. To keep the links manageable, wrap 1-foot (30.5-centimeter) sections of wire around your dowel rod or mandrel at a time.

2. Using two pairs of pliers, close half of the rings. True up your connection by gently squeezing the jaws of the flat-nose pliers over the seam.

3. Place the closed rings in rows on your flameproof soldering surface. Arrange the rings so the joins point towards you. Brush the joins of the rings with flux.

These rows of silver jump rings are ready to be soldered.

4. Place one chip of hard solder on each join. Heat the area around the ring with your torch until the solder flows, and then move on to the next ring.

5. Quench the rings in water.

6. Take two of the closed rings and connect them with one of the open rings. Use the two pairs of pliers, and make sure the ends meet flush.

7. Line up the three-ring unit on your soldering surface, with the open portion of the middle jump ring to the front, pointing towards you. Brush only the middle ring with flux. Use a tiny chip of solder.

8. Direct the flame straight down and towards the front of the unit, taking care not to overheat the two already-soldered outer rings. Use cross-lock tweezers to hold the already-soldered rings out of the way if needed.

9. Solder groups of three rings until all of the soldered links from the initial round of soldering have been used up.

10. Take two groups of three rings and connect them with an open ring. Repeat the soldering operation to join them. Continue grouping rings and soldering them in this way until your chain is the length you want.

11. Pickle the chain, neutralize it, rinse it, and dry it.

Your chain is complete! You can make your own handmade clasp for your chain using the instructions in the next section.

Solder groups of silver rings to make a chain.

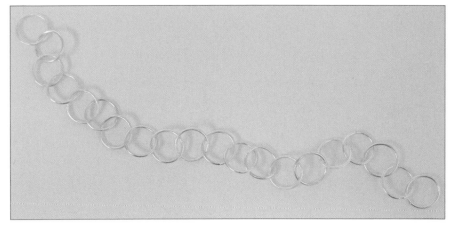

This completed silver links chain has been cleaned with a brass brush, water, and a few drops of Dawn dishwashing liquid.

Closures and Clasps

The best clasps are easy to work, feel comfortable when worn, and are beautiful to behold. A lot of types of clasps take hours to do and some precise engineering. These complex clasps can become part of your jewelry-making repertoire in time. For now, let's start with something simple and beautiful.

You can make an S-clasp with the following step-by-step instructions. Use annealed copper, brass, or sterling silver wire. Fine silver will be too soft to hold the shape. Note that this project also calls for a planishing hammer with a polished face. A ball-peen hammer will work, but any texture on the face of the hammer will transfer to your clasp.

You need the following supplies to make an S-clasp:

- About 2½ inches (6.25 centimeters) of 14- or 16-gauge wire (you can use 18-gauge sterling silver for lightweight necklaces)
- Metal shears or cutting pliers
- Round-nose pliers
- Flat-nose pliers
- Steel bench block
- Planishing hammer with polished face

Follow these steps:

1. Place the cut wire on your steel bench block and hammer ¼ inch (.75 centimeters) of each end with your planishing hammer.

2. Grasp a flattened end of the wire in the flat-nose pliers and turn the end up slightly. Or you could use round-nose pliers to make a tiny loop instead. Repeat for the other flattened end, turning it the opposite way.

3. Place the jaws of your round-nose pliers about ½ inch (1.25 centimeters) from the end of the wire. Hold the wire in the largest part of the round nose, close to the jaw. Push the wire around the pliers using your thumb, creating ½ of the S shape.

4. Place the other end of the wire in your pliers. Roll it around the jaws of the pliers the opposite direction, completing the *S* shape. Adjust the opening so a jump ring can be placed in one end.

5. Place the clasp on your steel bench block and lightly hammer the curved portions of the S shape to work-harden them and create dimension. Avoid hammering the turned-up ends. File and sand the clasp as needed to remove any marks.

You can change up the look of the S-clasp by choosing square wire that has been twisted. Change the look even more dramatically by making one end of the S very small and the other end into a larger C-shape. Enjoy the possibilities offered by this one basic style of closure.

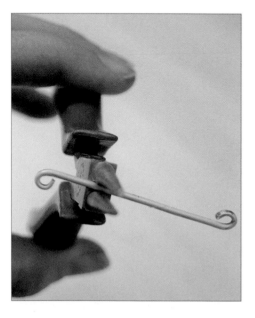

Position the round-nose pliers on the silver wire before bending it into the S shape.

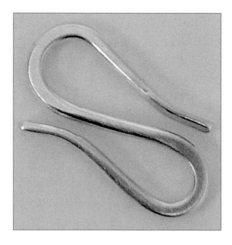

This dimensional sterling necklace clasp is complete.

Bails and End Caps

Bails are the part of a pendant that serves as a means of attachment to a necklace. *End caps* are the terminations used at either end of a necklace. They serve as a means to attach a clasp or closure. Just as with all of the findings available to jewelry makers, a million different available styles serve the same basic purpose.

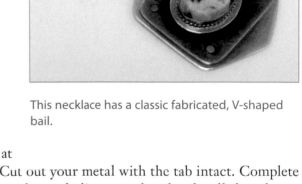

This necklace has a classic fabricated, V-shaped bail.

Bail Styles

The three key styles of bails are a jump ring, an integral bail, and a fabricated bail. A simple jump ring, sized appropriately to the scale of the project, can be used to attach a pendant to a necklace. The ring can be soldered closed for security.

An *integral bail* is fun to design into your pendant projects. To do this, allow extra metal at the top of your pendant design, creating a tab. Cut out your metal with the tab intact. Complete all of the work on your pendant. Then, using round-nosed pliers or a dowel rod, roll the tab over to create the bail. You can roll it forward or backward, depending on the style you like best.

A *fabricated bail* is created separately from the main pendant. It is then soldered or riveted to the pendant. The bail can be cut from sheet or made from wire. Design possibilities abound in the area of bails.

End Cap Styles

End caps are used at the ends of necklace chains or cords. They create a small loop for hooking your clasp into. Or the loop can hold a slightly larger jump ring for hooking your clasp into. They can be attached with solder or glued in with two-part epoxy. They also can be attached mechanically by crimping coiled wire around the cord or necklace. The last coil on the end is pulled open, and it serves to secure a clasp or another finding.

You can make your own basic coil end cap for use on chain or cord necklaces. Choose annealed copper, brass, or sterling silver wire for your coil. Make sure the wire size you select is compatible with the scale of the cord you're using. Usually, 18- or 20-gauge wire is a good choice.

The sample project uses 18-gauge square wire wound around a 3-millimeter dowel for a 3-millimeter diameter woven leather cord necklace. You need the following tools and supplies to make this basic coil end cap for yourself:

- About 8 inches (20.25 centimeters) of 18-gauge wire
- 3-millimeter dowel rod
- Cutting pliers or fine-point scissors
- Flat-nose and chain-nose pliers

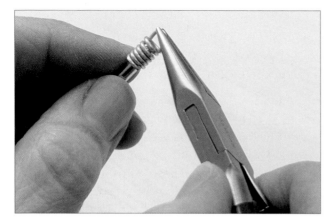

Use chain-nose pliers to pull up a wire coil to create an end cap.

Use pliers to attach a clasp to the coil end cap.

- Fine-point permanent marker
- 6-inch ruler
- Optional: Devcon 30-Minute two-part epoxy, 400-grit wet/dry sandpaper

Here's what to do:

1. Wrap your annealed wire around the dowel rod. When wrapping is complete, remove the coil.

2. Measure to the center of the coil, and mark it using the marker. Cut the coil into two pieces using cutting pliers or scissors.

3. Place one of the coils on the dowel rod. Gently wedge the tip of the pliers in between the two loops closest to the end of the dowel rod. Open out the last loop, turning it at a 90-degree angle to the coil. Remove this coil, and repeat with the other coil.

4. Thread one coil onto one end of the cord. Adjust the cord so its cut end is located deep inside the coil, near the looped end.

   Optional: Mix the two-part epoxy and dip the cord end into the glue before inserting the cord into the coil.

5. Place your chain-nose pliers over the loop that is the farthest from the end of the coil. Squeeze down on that loop, gently compressing it against the cord to secure it. Wipe off any excess glue, if you're using it.

6. Smooth any marks in the coil using 320-grit wet/dry sandpaper. Repeat the steps to create an end cap for the other end of the cord.

You now have two coil end caps on your cord necklace. Attach a clasp at one end and a jump ring at the other end, and you'll have a completed necklace.

Pin and Brooch Mechanisms

Pin back findings are added to the reverse side of a brooch to allow it to attach to clothing. You can purchase commercial pin back findings. Soldering the pin assembly onto your brooch is the last soldering operation you'll do on a project, so plan your entire project accordingly.

A popular commercial pin finding includes three components: a catch that opens and closes, a pin stem, and a hinge to capture the pin stem. The pin catch and hinge are soldered to the brooch with the hinge on the right for a right-handed user. The pin stem is placed into the hinge to complete the set. The whole thing is generally placed toward the upper third of a brooch, to keep it from flopping forward while being worn. An exception to this placement can be seen in the fabricated pin project in Chapter 14. Due to the narrowness of the brooch, the pin stem is placed vertically rather than horizontally.

You can solder a pin finding using the following step-by-step guide. If your metal is an inch or less in size, you can use a small butane torch to do the job.

To solder a three-piece pin finding to your work, you need these tools and supplies:

- Your brooch
- Your three-piece pin catch assembly (check the catch to make sure it's working properly)
- Fine-point permanent marker
- Torch setup
- Pickle pot with pickle solution, neutralizing bath, and plain water bath
- Brass brush
- Heatproof surface and flameproof soldering surface
- Easy solder

- Solder pick
- Paste flux
- Flux brush or small artist's brush
- Fine-point tweezers
- Copper tongs
- Chain-nose pliers
- Number 2 flat hand file
- 320-grit wet/dry sandpaper
- Clean hand towel or paper towels
- Dirt

A pin finding consists of a catch, a pin stem, and a hinge.

Start with clean metal, and then follow these steps:

1. On the back of the brooch, measure ¼ inch (6.25 millimeters) down from the top, and use the marker to draw a horizontal line. Try not to touch the clean metal with your fingers, only the marker. Mark two vertical lines a quarter-inch from the right and left edges. The two spots where these lines intersect indicates the soldering position of the pin catch and pin hinge.

2. Open and close the catch part of the pin catch to make sure it works well. Leave the pin catch in the open position.

3. Take a tiny piece of dirt, grit, sand, or pumice and stick it in the open mouth of the pin catch. This material will prevent solder from flowing up into the catch.

4. Lightly sand the bottom of the catch and the hinge.

5. Apply flux in a thin, even layer to the bottom only of the catch and the hinge. Holding the pieces in your tweezers may help you do this. Set both of the pieces on their sides on your soldering surface.

6. Apply a thin, even layer of paste flux right over the marks you made on the back of the brooch. Set the brooch on your soldering surface.

7. Use tweezers to place the pin hinge on the right side of your brooch, directly over the intersection of the two marks. Use tweezers to place two small pallions of easy silver solder on either side of the pin hinge. The solder chip must make a little bridge between the hinge and the brooch. Do the same thing with the pin catch, only place it just slightly above the intersection on the left side of the brooch. The open jaw of the pin catch points downward.

8. Light the torch. Swirl the flame a few times around brooch. Then move the flame back and forth over the middle of the brooch. The water contained in the flux will begin to boil off at about 200 degrees. This action could move your solder chips around. Keep your pick at the ready to move them back into place.

9. When the flux turns clear, you can move the torch flame closer, but not directly on the small pin parts. Keep the flame moving in a circular motion around the pin hinge. When you see the silver flash of melting solder, immediately move the flame away from that area. Repeat this process for the pin catch.

SAFE 'SMITHING

Before lighting your torch, take a look around you. Have you removed any paper towels or flammable items from the area? These often get left near the soldering station.

10.   Let the brooch air-cool for five minutes before quenching it. This is a safety precaution because the pin assembly is delicate.

11.   Pickle the metal for five minutes. Then neutralize and rinse it in plain water and lightly clean it using a brass brush.

12.   Gently twist the pin catch and hinge to make sure they have been soldered securely.

13.   Put the brooch face down on a piece of cloth or paper toweling on your work surface. Place the pin stem into the pin hinge. Place the jaws of the chain-nose pliers over the hinge and lightly squeeze.

14.   If the pin stem is too long, trim it with cutting pliers. The end of the pin should come just inside the edge of your brooch back. File and sand the edges to a smooth point.

A hinge is being soldered on this brooch back.

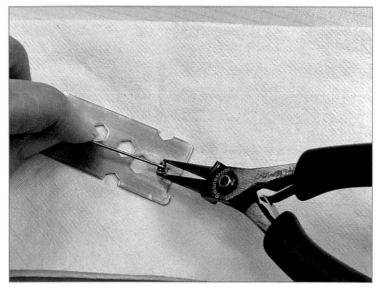

Use chain-nose pliers to secure the pin stem in the pin hinge.

> **METAL MISHAP**
>
> If you need to resolder, gently clean the metal with a brass brush. Make sure the catch still works, and remember to put some grit into the jaws of the catch to keep solder from flowing into it. Then apply flux again and resolder.

Ear Wires

You can make your own ear wires simply and easily. The length can be customized, too.

To make one pair of ear wires, you need these materials:

- Two 2- to 3-inch (5- to 7.5-centimeter) pieces of 20-gauge sterling silver wire with the ends sanded smooth
- Smooth-jaw pliers: round and flat nose
- Steel bench block
- Ball-peen or planishing hammer with smooth face
- Dowel rod, ink pen, or mandrel for wire wrapping, about ½ inch (1.25 centimeters) in diameter

To make the ear wires, follow these steps:

1. Using the flat-nose pliers, grasp one of the pieces of wire about ¼ inch (6.25 millimeters) from the end. Turn the wire at a 90-degree angle, creating a bend. Repeat for the second ear wire.

2. Switch to the round-nose pliers. Grasp the end of the bent wire midway in the jaws of your pliers. Grab only the end of the wire. Roll the pliers around, making a small loop. Repeat for the second ear wire.

3. Shape the ear wire on your mandrel. Hold the mandrel in your nondominant hand, and hold the small loop you just made against the mandrel. Wrap the wire around the mandrel, creating a larger loop. Repeat for the second ear wire.

4. Hold on to the back of one of the ear wires with your dominant hand. Hold the small front loop and the mandrel with your nondominant hand. Pinch the back of the ear wire with your thumb and first finger. Pull it down and away from the mandrel once or twice, allowing your fingers to slide over and smooth the wire and create a curved "leg" to the back of the ear wire. Repeat with other ear wire.

5. Place both ear wires on the mandrel, side by side, and compare them for shape and length. Make any adjustments before proceeding to the next step.

6. Place an ear wire on a steel bench block. With the flat face of your polished hammer, lightly tap all over the surface of the ear wire to work-harden it. It helps to hold onto the tail and the loop end at the same time to maintain the shape while you're hammering. Repeat this process with the second ear wire.

Bend wire over a mandrel to create an ear wire.

Check that the ear wires are the same length. Make adjustments as needed. You can trim the length of the ear wires to suit your taste. Sand any cut edges smooth using 400-grit wet/dry sandpaper before wearing them.

To change up the look of your ear wires, try these techniques:

- Use less wire and a smaller mandrel to create a smaller-size ear wire.

- Make crescent-shaped ear wires. After making the small loop, wrap the ear wire around a 1-inch mandrel. Remove the mandrel and bend the wire at the halfway point using flat-nose pliers.

- Use thinner 22-gauge wire for earring designs with smaller, more delicate dangles. Use heavier 19-gauge wire to make a bolder, more dramatic statement.

- Solder a sphere of silver or other decorative element just above the small loop on the ear wire.

You can get just as elaborate as your imagination can take you when you have a foundation of basic knowledge in making your own jewelry findings.

Finishing Touches

In This Chapter

- How to polish jewelry by hand and with power tools
- How to seal your work with wax or varnish
- How to clean your jewelry
- How to remove tarnish

I hope you've had the chance to make a metal jewelry project by now, and you want to put on the finishing touch. Or maybe you want to try some test finishes to see how things will turn out before committing your metal to a full-blown project. It might even be that you have a few older pieces of jewelry in your jewelry box. Could they be shined up and brought back to life?

Read on to learn ways to polish and seal your jewelry, taking into account any patina that you have previously applied. Get information on waxes and sealers, and find out how to use them properly—if at all. Even finished and sealed jewelry changes over time, but you can keep your jewelry looking its best with the tips presented in this chapter.

Polishing Your Work

Learning how to finish your jewelry adds another skill to your technique toolbox. This skill builds on earlier strategies, such as filing and sanding. In many cases, polishing is just refined sanding. The finesse you've shown in those earlier techniques will radiate once your work is polished and sealed. As with so many aspects of metalsmithing, the little things you do in the last step count. The sum total can elevate your work to the point of elegance. With polishing, you can transform even simply made jewelry to long-lasting items of worth that you are proud to wear or give.

Keep in mind that a good finish starts with a good foundation. Before you polish, take a moment to review your work. Look closely for any unnoticed dings or damage. Run your fingers over every millimeter to check for sharp edges or points. Try on your jewelry to make sure it doesn't catch on hair or clothing and that all clasps, hooks, or wires are in good working order. Go back to do any needed filing or sanding before proceeding.

With your fabrication work done, you're ready to put the final finish on your jewelry project. You have lots of choices to make your jewelry shine. In the following sections, I focus on finishing work by hand, but I also touch upon using power tools, such as a flexible shaft machine or a tumbler filled with stainless steel shot, peppered with a word or two regarding polishing compounds.

Sample Hand-Polishing Progression

Once you have checked that your jewelry is in tip-top condition, you can proceed with a basic polishing job using sandpapers or polishing papers. Gather some wet/dry sandpaper in 400 or 500 grits and cut it to the size you need for easy handling.

Rub all metal parts of your work with 400- or 500-grit sandpaper, running the paper in one direction only in straight lines traveling back and forth. You can do this either with or without water. Adding water is less aggressive and gives a softer finish. Avoid any gemstones or other embellishments.

After sanding, you can do some other things to affect the appearance of your jewelry. If you want a shinier appearance, use a fine, soft polishing paper; 3M makes a variety of these. (Read more about them in Chapter 7.) Cut the large sheet to size with scissors, and use it wet or dry to achieve a soft glow.

If you'd prefer a light, all-over textured finish, you can use a brass-bristle brush, natural-bristle brush, a piece of suede or denim, a green scrubbing pad, or steel wool applied in a swirling, overlapping motion or a straight back-and-forth motion. Find out more about these options in Chapter 9.

Polishing Compounds

Polishing compounds are natural or man-made abrasives mixed with a waxy binder that are available in sticks or bars and applied by hand or machine. Polishing compounds, like sandpapers, are traditionally applied in progression from most to least abrasive. Some metalsmiths like the sequence of using Tripoli first, then White Diamond, and then a rouge compound, such as red rouge, to polish metal to a bright shine. Choose your polishing compounds from a single supplier until you familiarize yourself with their properties under your use.

To polish metal with a polishing compound, start with very clean metal and thoroughly wash and dry your metal between every change of compound. To apply the compound, rub the compound onto a polishing stick or hold it against a slowly spinning wheel. Now your applicator is "charged" with compound. Err on the side of less compound rather than more.

To polish your metal with polishing sticks charged with compound, buff your metal vigorously to your desired shine. If you are using a polishing wheel in a flexible shaft machine, wear goggles or a face shield and a dust mask or respirator. Grip the metal firmly in your nondominant hand. Gently apply the spinning wheel to your work and run the wheel over the high points.

There are a few drawbacks to a bright, shiny finish. In the process of finishing your metal, sometimes you will uncover fire stain or firescale. If you yearn for that mirror finish, this will have to be removed via filing and sanding before you can proceed. Another common problem is one of overfinishing and losing some of the fine detail you've worked to create. Finally, highly reflective mirror finishes are very prone to scratching and will need repolishing to maintain the shine.

ARTISAN TIP

Try making your own polishing sticks to achieve a glossy shine on your metal. Follow the steps to make sanding sticks in Chapter 7. Instead of sandpaper, glue strips of leather, felt, or suede to your sticks. Each stick must be dedicated to one type of polishing compound. Buff your metal vigorously to your desired shine. Wash metal well with Dawn and lots of water in between each type of compound. You can also use polishing sticks without any compound.

Power Tool Polishing

If you want to add a new item to your toolkit, a tumble polisher comes in handy. It gives a bright, polished shine and also work-hardens your jewelry. However, it doesn't remove gouges or deep scratches, and it can't be used on jewelry containing gemstones. Your work also needs to be prepared properly before it goes into the tumbler, just as it does before you add any final polish. To use the tumble polisher, add stainless steel shot, water to just cover the shot, and one drop of Dawn dishwashing liquid to the barrel. Put in your jewelry, turn it on, and let it run for an hour to several hours.

If you have access to a flexible shaft machine or a Dremel tool, you can use a variety of polishing wheels to finish your metal. Always go slow when using motorized tools to do any jewelry-making task.

The barrel of this tumble polisher is filled with stainless steel shot, water and detergent, and jewelry.

This wood holder contains various bits and burs for a flex shaft.

Wire wheels and crazy hairs are useful polishing tools.

SAFE 'SMITHING

You might wonder why I don't mention the motorized polishing wheel as a finishing option. A spinning wheel of fabric seems innocent enough. Perhaps that's why it's dangerous. Jewelry can easily be grabbed and flung at high speed across the room. It can damage jewelry or harm innocent living things. It can yank loose clothing, hair, or fingers into the moving parts. Polishing particulate becomes airborne and can irritate skin, eyes, and lungs. If you use this equipment, practice all appropriate safety measures, including using dedicated vacuum equipment and wearing safety glasses, and keep children or pets out of the room while using it.

The following are a few good flex shaft polishing wheels to try. You can use these in a Dremel tool, also.

Crazy hairs. Their proper name is 3M radial bristle discs. They are frilly rubber wheels impregnated with ceramic aluminum oxide polishing compound. They are available in an assortment of grits. You don't need to add any polishing compound, and they aren't messy to use. Use three to five of these on a screw mandrel, and stack them so they point in the same direction. For long-lasting bristles, consider the direction of the rotation of the flex shaft. The bristles should lie naturally against the surface to be polished, spinning with the direction of the bristles instead of against them. I like the peach-colored, 6-micron disc size. They look a bit wild, hence the nickname crazy hairs.

Muslin or felt wheels. You can use these wheels by themselves or with red rouge or any other jewelry polishing compound. Each compound should be dedicated to a single wheel. Wash your work with liquid Dawn and water between any changes of compound.

Wire wheels. These are found in brass and steel and come in multiple sizes and shapes. Match the color of the wire wheel to the color of your metal.

Polishing and finishing my work by hand gives me a great deal of pleasure. I like going over the details of what I've done one last time. The action is rather meditative. I hope you find the same thing as you finish your jewelry.

Preserving the Finish

Exposure to sunlight, moisture, detergents, chemicals, and the wear-and-tear of daily living will make their mark on your wearable art. You have worked diligently to create your jewelry project, so you should spend a little time to protect its finish. The best time to do that is after you've polished your work.

Sealing metal with an applied wax or a spray varnish helps to preserve the finish. It will extend the life of your applied patinas and will protect delicate patinas from flaking. It protects metal from fingerprints, dirt, and grime through the use of a protective coating. The coating, which varies in strength, durability, and thickness, seals out some of the effects of the environment. Moisture and pollution in the air can change the look of the metal's surface in ways you might not want. Sealers and waxes prevent unwanted tarnish. And they make cleaning jewelry easier down the road.

You have many choices as far as ways to protect your metal. There are several sealers and waxes that are easy to apply, work consistently, and have good preservation qualities. In the following sections, I review the details of some good options for you to try.

A leaf pendant with a fragile blue green patina, protected with several very light layers of clear matte acrylic spray sealer.

Choosing a Wax or a Varnish

The two main types of sealers for metal are waxes and varnishes. Waxes can be plant, animal, petroleum, or synthetic, or a blend of these. Varnishes can be a resin mixed with oil, or they can be an acrylic polymer emulsion. Most jewelry makers who use a varnish opt for a spray-on, clear, acrylic variety. Be prepared to repeat the protective layer over time.

What both types of sealers have in common is their film-forming abilities. How that film is applied, how it affects the finish or patina you have applied, and how it performs over time are what sets them apart. I go into all of that here, with information on waxes first, followed by acrylic varnishes.

The first wax used in preserving jewelry was beeswax, and it's still used today. The time-consuming method of melting the wax and coating jewelry and then buffing seems to have lost favor over time, though many seasoned metalsmiths still use it. You can, too, if you like.

In the meantime, other wax-bearing products have been developed for protecting things such as floors, cars, and the British Crown jewels. They can protect your treasured metal items, too. A couple of winners in the wax category are

- **SC Johnson Paste Wax.** This blend of carnauba, paraffin, and microcrystalline waxes was created to protect wood floors.
- **Renaissance Micro-Crystalline Wax Polish.** This proprietary blend of microcrystalline waxes was developed by the British Museum to protect its collections.

> **ARTISAN TIP**
>
> All waxes and varnishes will alter the finish you already have. There isn't a sealer out there that will not impact the color or look of your metal in some way. You will want to be prepared for that, so you don't coat your jewelry with something you'll hate. Of course, you also can choose to go sealer-free and allow nature to take its course.

Both of these waxes provide a clear, hard, water-resistant finish to jewelry. Both have been used by jewelry makers for years. Johnson Paste Wax has a good reputation for toughness and durability. Renaissance wax offers dimensional depth and warmth. However, it may not last as long as Johnson Paste Wax because it was designed to protect objects in museum environments, not worn on people's bodies.

Varnishes used to be oil based only. Over time, acrylic-based options became available, and that's what I recommend for sealing your metal jewelry. Acrylic spray varnishes are safer to use in protecting jewelry. They are easy to spray on and wear fairly well, too. Consider this type of sealer if you have a fragile patina, such as the green-blue one achieved with ammonia.

There's no particular brand that I recommend here. Instead, look for the type of finish you want, such as gloss, semi-gloss, or matte. Spray sealers leave a fairly shiny or glossy finish, even ones I've tried that are classified as matte finish. They also change the look of your patina and surface treatments. This change can be subtle or dramatic. I recommend that you experiment with several types of sprays to see which you like best.

Applying Waxes and Varnishes

Both wax-based sealers and spray varnishes are easy to apply. To apply a wax, use a tiny amount of wax on a soft, lint-free cloth. Rub it all over the metal. With Renaissance wax, you may immediately buff the surface vigorously to get a soft sheen. With Johnson Paste Wax, leave the wax on the surface for about 30 minutes, and then buff. You may add two to three coats of either wax, as desired. For little nooks and crannies, use an old, soft toothbrush.

To apply an acrylic spray varnish, wash metal with Dawn dishwashing detergent and rinse and dry the metal thoroughly. Take your item outside or to a well-ventilated area. Protect surroundings from overspray or place your work in a cardboard box. Follow the direction on the can for application. Be sure to start and stop the action of the spray when it is off of your metal. Use only very, very, very light coats and apply several of them. Allow drying time between coats. You can use very fine, 0000 steel wool in between the last coat or two to smooth the surface further. If your jewelry appears to have a powdery layer after you've sprayed it with varnish, you've sprayed it too thickly. Use the steel wool to rub it down.

Taking Care of Your Jewelry

Although the things you do to your metal seem like they should last forever, they don't. The amount of wear, environmental conditions, pollutants, and even body chemistry affect jewelry. Jewelry living in high humidity, pollution, or high-sulfur environments will have a reaction soonest. Heavy perspiration, detergents, and even lemon juice can get though a protective film and cause a patina to change or become bleached out. Even jewelry stuck away in an enclosed box isn't immune—it gets tarnished.

Don't let this information make you nervous about wearing the jewelry you've made or about giving it as gifts. You have worked hard to create your wearable design, and that's just what you should do—wear it. To my mind, daily living adds a patina of its own, one that can't be created any other way. It will keep tarnish away better than leaving the jewelry sitting in your jewelry box, too. Still, you'll want to know about ways to maintain jewelry, remove tarnish, or refresh a waxed or sealed finish.

Maintaining Your Jewelry

For routine maintenance of your jewelry, rinse your jewelry with plain water, and then add a drop of mild liquid hand soap. Suds it up using your fingers, or use an old toothbrush for dirty crevices. Rinse the jewelry with clear water, and then buff it dry with a soft cloth.

This hammered copper cuff bracelet with iridescent patina maintains its glow with a simple soap-and-water cleaning and buffing with a soft cloth.

This type of cleaning brings back a surprising luster to jewelry. It works like a charm! Note that you should do this only if the jewelry is water-resistant.

Removing Tarnish

One way to remove tarnish from jewelry is to use a yellow Sunshine Polishing Cloth, made specifically for polishing jewelry. Make sure jewelry is clean and free of dust or dirt first, and then rub the cloth over the surface until you get the shine you want. You can use the cloth until it is completely blackened. A similar option is a cloth impregnated with red rouge on one side and lined with a yellow flannel backing on the other side. Use the red rouge side to remove tarnish and clean your jewelry, and use the yellow side for a final polish.

METAL MISHAP

Using a polishing cloth on dusty or dirty jewelry will scratch the finish. I learned this lesson the hard way when I dry-buffed my high school boyfriend's Corvette convertible, making swirly scratches all over the body. And they didn't improve by rubbing them more, either. If your jewelry is dirty, simply get it wet, add a drop of mild liquid hand soap, rinse it, and buff with a soft, clean cloth.

Another option is to use one of the fine-grit 3M polishing papers to lightly polish and remove tarnish from jewelry. First, wash jewelry using the previous routine maintenance step, and then use the soft sandpaper to polish your jewelry.

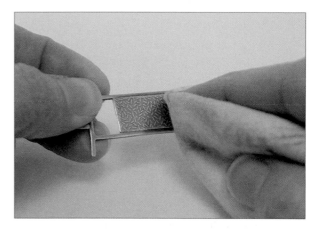

A Sunshine Polishing Cloth helps to shine a pendant.

If you don't have special polishing cloths or papers, you can try this old tarnish-removing remedy. Completely line a nonmetal baking dish with aluminum foil. In a saucepan, boil enough water to cover the jewelry in the foil-lined dish. Add a handful of baking soda, a good squirt of Dawn dishwashing liquid, and about ¼ teaspoon (1.25 milliliters) of salt to the water. When the salt is dissolved, carefully pour the solution over the jewelry in the foil-lined dish. Allow it to sit until water cools or jewelry appears brightened. Remove your items using a plastic spoon or other plastic utensil. Rinse your jewelry very well under cool running water and dry it with a clean, soft cloth. This method creates an electrolytic action, causing tarnish to fall away. It can be worth the effort if you have a great deal of tarnished jewelry to clean.

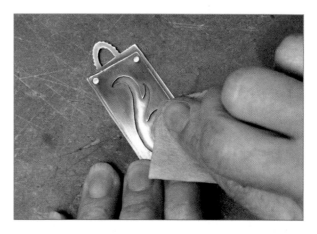

3M blue polishing paper restores shine to a pendant.

A tumble polisher also removes tarnish from jewelry. Use it as outlined in the previous section, "Power Tool Polishing." Let the tumbler run for about 30 minutes.

> **SAFE 'SMITHING**
>
> If you use a tarnish-removing dip, you need good ventilation. These dips are corrosive and remove bits of metal along with any tarnish they take away. They can damage delicate jewelry. Don't ever use them on pearls, turquoise, coral, or other soft gems. If you do use such a dip, it must make the briefest contact with jewelry. Afterward, rinse jewelry with plenty of water immediately. Buff with a clean, soft cloth.

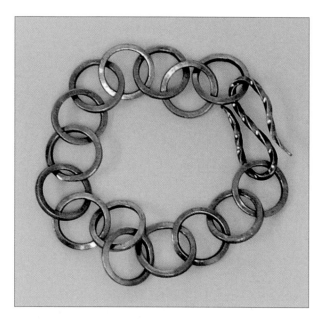

This bracelet is tarnished.

This is the same bracelet after being tumble-polished.

Reapplying Wax or Varnish

Eventually, you may want to reapply a wax or varnish. Other than cleaning jewelry first, there's no special preparation needed for reapplying wax. Old varnish needs to be removed before you can apply new varnish.

To reapply a wax finish, wash jewelry with hand soap, using the previous routine maintenance procedure. Using a clean, dry, soft cloth, reapply another coat or two of wax. You can reapply the same wax you used initially or switch to another type. Buff it using a clean portion of your cloth. That's it!

Removing and reapplying an acrylic varnish coating takes longer and is more complex. Tackle this process only if the coating is peeling or the jewelry has become very discolored, and routine maintenance with soapy water isn't helping.

To remove and reapply an acrylic sealer, follow these steps:

1. Use acetone and a soft cloth to remove clear acrylic coatings. Be sure to do this step in a well-ventilated area, and wear latex or rubber gloves.

2. The acetone might remove any patina that you have applied as well. If this is the case, reapply the patina.

3. Allow plenty of time for any wet patina to dry. For a liver of sulfur patina or an ammonia patina, allow it to cure overnight. You can seal a heat patina as soon as the metal has cooled.

4. Respray the acrylic sealer in a few quick, very light coats, as previously described in "Applying Waxes and Varnishes." Allow it to dry thoroughly.

Even though the reapplication of waxes and varnishes seems a bit laborious or time-consuming, it's not a burden. To make things easier, I lean toward a wax finish.

Enjoying the Natural Progression of Metal

I don't mind that the patina of my jewelry will change over time. It's part of the beauty of making and wearing metal jewelry. I have a simple forged copper cuff that I wear almost daily. It gets a bath every few weeks—more often in the summertime when I sweat! Occasionally, it receives a fresh coat of Renaissance wax. That's it. The raised edges of the bracelet have become burnished bright with wear while the inner recesses possess a rich, deep iridescent patina. No matter how many bracelets I make exactly like this one, each of them will always look and wear differently. I like that.

You may choose to allow your metal to gain its own patina over time. That's perfectly fine. You'll get to understand that metal really is organic, and the things we do to it to call it finished are only the beginning of the journey it takes over time.

Creating Metal Jewelry: 10 Projects

In This Chapter

- Two pairs of earrings
- Three pendants
- Two bracelets
- A necklace, a set of cuff links, and a brooch

The 10 projects in this chapter are ordered from approachable to challenging based upon both tools and techniques needed to complete them. Two more projects are waiting online for you at idiotsguides.com/metaljewelry. I give you ways to customize the projects, too, making them your own. Go ahead, unleash your genius!

During your test drive of the projects, remain open to the experimental nature your journey. Everything won't go exactly as expected. It never does! Celebrate that you've taken this step and embrace all you will learn. At the end of each exploration, you'll have jewelry that no one else on earth has. The fact that you made it with your own two hands, your head, and your heart is its own reward.

Basic Setups for the Projects

This chapter brings you a mashup of projects to get your creative engine going. But you need to make sure you have a full tank before pulling out of the driveway. Check to see that you have all of the materials you need, plus a little bit more.

There are several basic setups for the projects, along with some specialty tools. To prepare you for the projects, please review the lists included here. Each project will include the name of the basic setups you'll need under "Setups," along with any specialty tools you'll need.

Torch setup:

- Butane, all-in-one, plumber's, or jeweler's torch
- Pickle solution
- Pickle pot (small slow cooker)
- Copper tongs
- Two containers of water, one for quenching and one with 3 tablespoons (44.25 milliliters) of baking soda mixed in for neutralizing
- Flameproof soldering surface
- Heatproof surface (baking pan for butane torch, cement backer board or kiln bricks for larger torches)
- Fine-point, stainless steel tweezers
- Insulated grip, cross-lock tweezers
- Paste flux
- Natural-bristle artist's brush (inexpensive)
- Small plastic carton with holes drilled in bottom (for pickle pot)
- Assortment of silver solders in hard, medium, and easy
- Striker
- Soldering props and helpers, such as steel t-pins, nickels, binding wire, and bits of broken ceramic honeycomb block
- Fire extinguisher

Pliers setup:

- Flat nose
- Round nose
- Chain nose
- Flat/half-round forming
- Hole-punching

Forging and forming setup:

- Ball-peen hammer (unpolished)
- Planishing or ball-peen hammer (polished)
- Forging hammer (polished)
- Rawhide mallet
- Stainless steel bench block

Forming tools setup:

- Ring mandrel
- Bracelet mandrel
- Dapping block and punches
- $\frac{3}{8}$ inch-wide (1 centimeter), $\frac{1}{2}$ inch-wide (1.25 centimeter), and $\frac{7}{8}$ inch-wide (2.25 centimeter) dowel rods in 12-inch lengths

Cutting and piercing setup:

- Jeweler's saw
- Saw blades, size 2/0, 3/0, and 6/0
- Metal shears
- Cutting pliers
- Scissors
- Center punch
- Bench pin and clamp
- Hand drill, drill press, electric drill, or flexible shaft machine
- Assortment of small drill bits

Filing, sanding, and finishing setup:

- Number 2 flat file
- Number 2 half-round ring file
- Number 3 barrette file
- Wet/dry sandpapers in 220, 320 and 400 grits
- Brass bristle brush
- Green scrubbing pad, such as Scotchbrite
- Fine steel wool

Stamping setup:

- Alphabet stamps
- 3-inch (7.5-centimeter) framing nail (spike)
- Masonry nails
- Circles template

Patina setup:

- Liver of sulfur, lump or gel form
- Ammonia (nonsudsy)
- Table salt
- Sawdust
- Plastic resealable bag
- Water
- Length of wire for dipping hook

Stone-setting setup:

- Burnisher
- Bezel pusher
- Toothbrush with head cut off or 6 inches (15.25 centimeters) of horn, cut at an angle and sanded smooth
- Twist ties
- Post-it notes
- Double-stick tape

Utility setup:

- 6-inch (15.25-centimeter) metal file with inch and metric measurements
- Sliding brass gauge or a digital caliper
- Fine-point and ultra fine-point permanent markers
- Degreasing liquid detergent, such as Dawn
- Dividers with two pointed ends
- Rubber cement or glue stick

Safety setup:

- Safety goggles
- Gloves
- Fan/ventilation
- Work apron

Optional: anvil, bench vise, masking tape, magnification headgear

This Ginger hammered, sterling silver, wire necklace features the Captured Canyon pendant.

(© Paul D'Andrea)

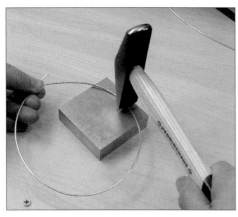

Hammer a circular wire shape.

Ginger Forged Necklace

This slim, forged, silver neck wire adds spice to any of the project pendants or stands up quite well on its own. Its strength and sparkle come from the hammer texture you apply. You can make the neck wire with heavier wire if you want, but then you must choose a heavier hammer to move your metal.

Materials: 17 inches (43.25 centimeters) of 16-gauge round sterling silver wire, annealed.

Setups: Pliers, utility, filing and sanding, plus rawhide mallet and polished planishing hammer or ball-peen hammer.

Follow these steps:

1. Hold both ends of wire in your nondominant hand. Starting ½ inch (1.25 centimeters) from one end, gently hammer one course along the length of the wire, keeping the bench block under your metal as you move the metal under the hammer. Keep the hammer level with the work surface and try to keep hammer blows centered over the middle of the wire. The metal will bend in crazy ways. This is normal.

2. Using your fingers, bend the wire into a round necklace shape. Hammer a second course along the wire in slightly overlapping blows.

3. Reshape the wire again, and add another course of light hammer blows.

4. Place ½ inch of one of the ends of the neck wire on the bench block. Hammer the wire, flattening it on the end. Turn the neck wire around, and flatten the other end. File the ends of the metal using the number 2 flat file.

5. Turn the ends of the wire to create hooks. Grasp the wire ½ inch from one edge using your round-nose pliers. Turn the wire around the pliers,

creating a hook shape. Bend ¼ inch (.75 centimeter) of the hook upward at the end. Repeat for the other side. You may need to use flat-nose pliers to turn one of the hooks so that the hooks meet at an offset angle as shown in the project photo. Keep in mind that you may need to make adjustments to the hooked ends to allow one end to pass through a pendant bail.

6. Clasp the hooks together and tug gently in opposite directions. This action adds the tension needed to keep the neck wire closed when it is worn.

7. Open the neck wire in a sideways motion, and put it around your neck. Clasp the hooks. Press the neck wire down and use your fingers to make final adjustments for a custom fit.

8. Remove the neck wire and apply two coats of wax, buffing in between coats.

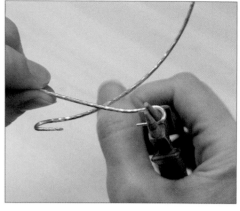

Use round-nose pliers to make a hook shape in the wire.

Glow Forged Copper Cuff Bracelet

Hammer work is a great way to release tension. Try this project after a hard day at the office. The next day you'll be wearing a smile and a stress-reducing copper bracelet on your wrist. In this project, you learn to anneal metal, cut heavy wire, and forge copper. Select your heaviest hammer for this project. A ball-peen hammer was used on the sample bracelet, but a larger forging hammer makes moving the metal much easier. Feel free to change the bright finish by adding a patina of your own choosing. You can customize the fit by adding or subtracting to the measurement of the wire.

Materials: 5¾ inches (14.5 centimeters) of 4-gauge copper wire.

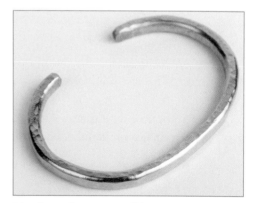

This forged copper cuff bracelet is a little less than ¼-inch (.75 centimeter) wide and about 6 inches (15.25 centimeters) around.

(© Paul D'Andrea)

> **ARTISAN TIP**
>
> This project takes only about an hour to complete using the high heat of a jeweler's torch. If you have a butane torch, choose a smaller gauge of copper wire, such as 12 or 14 gauge, to make annealing the metal easier.

Setups: Torch; filing, sanding, and finishing; plus jeweler's saw and number 2/0 blades, bench pin, forging hammer or ball-peen hammer, rawhide mallet, and bracelet mandrel or anvil.

Follow these steps:

1. Round the cut ends of your wire using a number 2 flat file. Smooth them using sandpapers, starting with 220 grit, then using 320 grit, and finishing with 400 grit. Pound the wire flat with the mallet.

2. Anneal your wire until it is bright orange. Immediately quench it in cold water, using your copper tongs. Remove it and dry it well. You will need to anneal your metal about three or four more times as you shape it, but don't pickle it to remove the oxides until the end.

3. Place your wire on the bench block or anvil and create the hammer texture. Start at the top of the wire and hammer one full course, and then turn the metal around and hammer another. Feed the metal under the hammer—keeping your fingers clear, of course.

4. Continue hammering until the pattern pleases you, and then anneal your metal and quench it.

5. Begin shaping the ends of your metal. Place about 1 inch (2.5 centimeters) of your metal on the horn of your anvil or on the bracelet mandrel. Using your rawhide mallet, form a wide hook on one end of the wire.

6. Flip the metal around so you're working the other end of the wire, and create a hook on that end, too. You should have a broad wire with a hook at either end. Use your hands to make adjustments so the hooks are even with each other. If the metal is too stiff to move with your hands, place it on your work surface and use the rawhide mallet to true up the shape.

> **ARTISAN TIP**
>
> Stop and look at your bracelet from time to time. To keep things in alignment, you can often make adjustments just by using your hands. If not, use the rawhide mallet to bring it back to shape. Always true up your shape before annealing the metal.

7. Refine the shape, working from the end of the bracelet to the middle. Then flip the bracelet so you can work it from the other end. Use your anvil or bracelet mandrel and the rawhide mallet to finish the rough form of the bracelet. If you are using the horn of an anvil, cup both ends of your bracelet in the palm of your hand. This will keep the bracelet in shape. If the metal isn't moving enough for you, switch back to your steel hammer.

8. Anneal the metal when it no longer responds to the hammer. Dry it well before reintroducing it to your tools. You'll want to pickle your metal after you anneal it for the last time.

9. Complete your forming with a final round of hammering with the rawhide mallet to work-harden the metal.

10. Smooth the inside of your completed bracelet with the number 2 half-round file, and then a series of wet/dry sandpapers, starting with 220 grit, then using 320 grit, and finishing with 400 grit. Don't sand the hammer marks on the outside of the bracelet.

11. Apply two coats of your choice of waxes to seal the copper.

Use a ball-peen hammer to form copper around an anvil horn.

Cup the ends of the bracelet in your hand to maintain the bracelet's shape when you use an anvil.

Heat your copper bracelet to orange hot with the torch to anneal it.

This pair of leaf-shaped earrings is colored with an easy-to-make patina.

Leaves Earrings with Blue-Green Patina

Be inspired by the natural simplicity of these earrings. The patina is easy, too. It's simply ammonia, salt, and sawdust. Feel free to change up the size and shape to suit your own image of nature.

Materials:

- 22- or 24-gauge sheet copper, approximately 3 × 3 inches (7.5 × 7.5 centimeters)

- Two sterling silver ear wires

Setups: Cutting and piercing; filing, sanding, and finishing; utility; patina (except for liver of sulfur); plus hole-punching pliers, bench block, a ⅞inch-wide (2.25 centimeters) dowel rod, paper for copying pattern, and spray matte acrylic sealer.

Follow these steps:

1. Make two copies of the pattern provided. Cut out the pattern, leaving a quarter-inch (.75 centimeter) border around the edges.

2. Clean your metal using 320-grit sandpaper. Then paste the pattern to your clean metal. Allow the paste to dry for a few minutes.

3. Using the jeweler's saw and a 3/0 blade, cut the leaves out of the metal. Remove the pattern by washing it off using your fingers and plenty of water.

4. File the edges using a flat file, and then smooth them with sandpaper.

5. Mark a spot for the ear wire near the top of each leaf shape. Use the hole-punching pliers to make small holes at these locations. Smooth any burs with sandpaper.

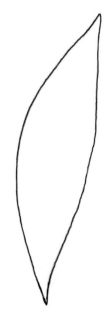

Make copies of this leaf pattern to create the Leaves earrings.

6. Place the leaves side by side, so you have a left and right side. Shape one of the leaves, using the dowel rod to assist you in making an undulating shape. Repeat for the other earring.

7. Clean the metal using Dawn and a brass brush or a green scrubbing pad. Dry with a soft cloth and set aside.

8. Prepare the patina by placing two cups of sawdust in a resealable plastic bag. Add enough ammonia to dampen all of the sawdust, approximately ½ cup (118.25 milliliters). Then add some table salt. Close the bag and knead everything together.

9. Open the bag and add the earrings, and then reclose it. Set the bag in a warm place for 24 hours.

10. Remove the earrings and rinse them lightly by swishing in clean water. Allow the earrings to dry. Once the earrings are completely dry, brush away any remaining sawdust.

11. Lightly sand the edges of the leaves using 400-grit sandpaper. Spray the leaves using several very light coats of clear acrylic sealer.

12. Allow the earrings to dry and then add the ear wires.

File the leaf shapes with a hand file.

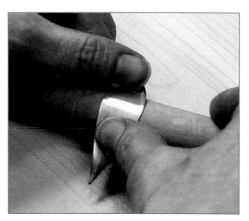
Shape the copper leaf over a dowel rod.

Tendril Pendant

Nature takes over in this simple circle shape with a twining tendril. The coil of the tendril creates an integral necklace bail. The coil reappears in the next project, where the tendril becomes a means to hold ear wires to a pair of earrings. The sample projects use brass, but you can use any metal you like. Practice making a few tendril shapes in thinner wire before beginning. Add a patina using the heat of a torch flame.

This brass open circle pendant features an integral necklace bail.

(© Paul D'Andrea)

The wire is coiled around the PVC pipe.

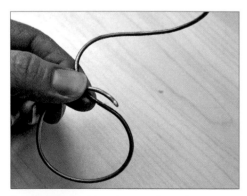

Form the wire into the pendant shape.

Materials: 12 inches (30.5 centimeters) of 14-gauge brass wire, annealed.

Setups: Torch (any torch); filing, sanding, and finishing; utility; plus polished hammer, metal shears, bench block, and 1¼-inch (3.25-centimeter) diameter PVC pipe.

Follow these steps:

1. Mark a spot 4 inches (10 centimeters) from one end of the annealed 14-gauge wire. Round the ends of the wire using the number 2 flat file, and then sand them smooth using 320- and 400-grit sandpapers. Reapply the marker if needed.

2. Wrap the wire around the PVC pipe to create a coil. Slide the coil off the pipe.

3. Make a 90-degree bend at the mark, bending the longer portion of wire up to make the coiled bail shape. At the other end of the wire, use round-nose pliers to make a small hook.

4. At the long end of the wire, use the round-nose pliers to create a coil of four loose loops. Pushing the wire around the jaws of the pliers using your free hand is helpful in moving the heavy material. This coil will be used as the bail, so make at least one of the loops large enough to accommodate a necklace. Anneal the wire as needed. Finish the coil by wrapping the hooked end and any remaining wire around the base of the pendant.

5. Adjust the coils at the top of the pendant using flat or chain-nose pliers. Check to make sure your necklace fits through one or two of the coils and is balanced. Use a half-round file to clean up marks left from pliers. Sand these areas as needed.

6. Apply the hammer texture to the base of the pendant using the ball end of a planishing hammer. Use the bench block under the pendant, with the coiled part of the pendant hanging over the edge.

7. Add a torch patina by placing the pendant on a flameproof surface and brushing the surface with the tips of your torch flame. Do this until the desired color is reached. Allow the pendant to air-cool.

8. Rub the surface of the pendant using fine steel wool, and then apply two coats of wax to seal it.

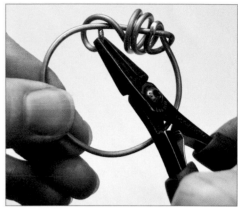

Use pliers to form the wire into the tendril shape.

Vine Earrings

Nature's work continues in this pair of earrings that coordinate beautifully with the pendant in the previous project. The tendril shape in these earrings creates an organic means of connecting the dangling elements to the ear wires. Practice making a few tendril shapes before beginning the project to get one that you like. The sample project uses brass for the dangles and sterling silver for the ear wires. You can add a patina to your dangles by using the heat of a torch flame.

Forge a pattern onto the tendril pendant using a hammer on a steel block.

Materials:

- 18 inches (45.75 centimeters) of 16-gauge brass wire, annealed

- Two sterling silver ear wires

- Two 8-millimeter sterling silver jump rings

Setups: Torch (any torch); filing, sanding, and finishing; utility; plus polished hammer, metal shears, bench block, and 1¼-inch (3.25-centimeter) diameter PVC pipe.

These brass open circle vine earrings coordinate with the previous pendant.

(© Paul D'Andrea)

Form a figure-eight coil.

Use round-nose pliers to form a small coil.

Follow these steps:

1. Wrap the annealed brass wire around the PVC pipe. Slide the coil off.

2. Mark a spot in the center of the coil. You may need to open the coil a little to do this. Cut it in half. Open the coils out so they look like a figure-eight. One side will be the hoop, and the other the tendril.

3. At the halfway point, bend a 90-degree leg in the wire using flat-nose pliers. Slightly straighten the wire using your fingers. This will make the tendril.

4. With the widest point of a pair of round-nose pliers, grasp the end of the tendril. Begin to wrap the wire around the pliers, making a coil. Use the tail of the coil to wrap around the lower part of the earring to secure it. Repeat the process with the other wire.

5. Put the earrings back on the PVC pipe to reshape them. Use the rawhide mallet to shape and work-harden the earrings, avoiding hammering the tendril areas.

6. Remove the earrings from the PVC pipe. Adjust the tendrils using flat-nose pliers.

7. Add the hammer texture. Place one of the earrings on the steel bench block, front side facing up, with the coiled area hanging over the side of the block. Hammer the hoop area to give it texture. Repeat the process for the second earring.

8. Add a torch patina if desired. Place the earrings on a flameproof surface and brush the surface with the tip of your torch flame. Do this until the desired color is reached. Allow the earrings to air-cool.

9. Rub the surface of the earrings using fine steel wool, and then apply two coats of wax to seal.

10. Attach jump rings and then ear wires to complete your earrings.

Paging Ms. Heroine Wide Copper Cuff Bracelet

Do you remember the last time you solved a tricky problem on your own? You figured it out for yourself. You became your own hero! Bring out the superhero in you with this simple, bold cuff. Learn a basic foldform while you're at it.

Materials: 6 × 2-inch (15.25 × 5-centimeter) piece of 22- or 24-gauge annealed copper.

Setups: Torch (all-in-one, plumber's, or jeweler's torch); filing, sanding, and finishing; utility; plus forging hammer, rawhide mallet, metal shears, bench block or anvil, bracelet mandrel, and bench vise.

Follow these steps:

1. File the four edges of the copper using the number 2 flat file. Sand the edges using 220-grit sandpaper.

2. Fold the metal in half, bringing the two short sides together. Squeeze them together as much as you can, using your fingers to adjust the alignment. Pound the fold flat using the rawhide mallet.

3. Switch to the forging hammer, and hammer all along the folded edge, using the wedge-shaped face of the hammer. Keep the hammer blows as close to the edge of the metal as you can, without hitting the bench block. You'll be holding the hammer at a slight angle to do this. Hammer on one side of the metal only. Do two courses of hammering using slightly overlapping blows.

4. Anneal the metal. Get it orange-hot and plunge it into water to quench. Dry the metal well.

5. Open the metal using your fingers, a cut-off toothbrush, or dull knife, and then use your mallet to flatten the metal out slightly.

This forged copper cuff has a crusty patina and a foldform design.

(© Paul D'Andrea)

Forging copper using a hammer on bench block.

A red vise holds the bench block on its side to stabilize it under the folded copper form that is being hit with a mallet.

Forge along the fold line on the cuff bracelet.

Use your hands and a bracelet mandrel held in a vise to form the bracelet.

6. Fold the metal in half again, this time along the long edge. Use your fingers to bring the edges together as before. Pound the piece of metal flat with the rawhide mallet.

7. Switch to the forging hammer, and hammer two to three courses along one side of the fold. Hammer close to the edge without allowing the hammer to contact the steel surface below, if possible.

8. Anneal the metal. Quench it, and then dry it well.

9. Pry the folded metal apart using a cut-off toothbrush or a dull knife. Open it all the way out using your fingers.

10. Use the forging hammer to hammer along the line of each of the opened folds. This action is known as "confirming the fold." Do two courses of hammering on each fold.

11. Place a bracelet mandrel in a bench vise. Place the end of the bracelet on the mandrel, and strike the metal with the mallet, using glancing blows towards you. Form a C-shape on the end. Form one side, and then flip the bracelet over to form the other side. Work your way to the middle to shape the rest of the bracelet, using both your hands and the rawhide mallet. You can hit the bracelet right on top of the folds, but take care when hitting just past the point of the fold. The raised area can dent easily.

12. Finish your cuff with a peanut oil patina (see Chapter 10) and two coats of wax.

I Love Lacy Pierced and Riveted Pendant

Combining two different metals adds depth and interest to your work. Take it further by adding a lacy pierced design. You decide if it reminds you of a favorite comedienne's updo.

Materials:

- 2½ × 1 inch (6.25 × 2.5 centimeters) of 24-gauge sterling silver sheet
- 2½ × 1 inch of 24-gauge copper sheet
- Four ¼-inch (6.25-millimeter) lengths of 14-gauge sterling silver round wire, annealed
- ⅜-inch (9.5-millimeter), 14-gauge jump ring

This silver and copper pendant has a pierced design.

(© Paul D'Andrea)

Setups: Torch (all-in-one, plumber's, or jeweler's torch); cutting and piercing; filing, sanding, and finishing; utility; plus goldsmith's hammer (or other hammer with a small, flat, polished face), pointed scribe or reamer, bench block, safety goggles, and paper.

Cut Out the Silver and Copper Patterns

To make the two pieces of this pendant, follow these steps:

1. Clean the copper and silver by sanding them with 400-grit sandpaper.

2. Make copies of the pattern provided. Cut out the pattern, leaving ¼ inch (.75 centimeter) border around the edges.

3. Paste the paper patterns onto both sheets of metal, allowing them to dry for a few minutes.

This is the pattern for the two pendant shape cutouts.

Saw the pattern out of the copper.

Saw the pattern out of the silver.

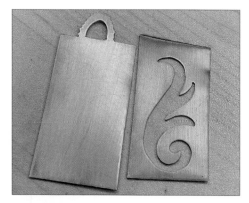

Silver and copper pendant parts.

4. Drill a small hole in the copper to allow the saw blade inside the pattern. Drill one hole in the silver, inside the bail.

5. Load the saw with a 3/0 (or finer) saw blade, and tighten one of the nuts on the saw frame. Thread the loose end of the blade through the drilled hole in the copper piece. Place the end of the blade into the other nut on the saw frame and tighten it.

6. Position your metal so it is supported by the bench block and begin to saw. Travel the saw blade slowly on the points and sharp curves.

7. When you finish sawing the copper piece, release one end of the saw blade, remove the blade, and rethread it into the drilled hole in the silver piece.

8. Saw out the interior shape of the bail on the silver piece. Then saw around the exterior of the bail.

9. After piercing out all of the interior shapes and the bail, use metal shears to trim away excess material from the outside of the pattern lines.

10. Use needle files to clean and refine the interior shapes. Use the number 2 flat file to refine outer shapes.

11. Sand both sides of the copper piece using 220-grit sandpaper. Then concentrate on sanding the front of the metal, using 320-grit and then 400-grit sandpapers, traveling in one direction while sanding. Repeat this step on the silver piece.

Rivet the Pieces Together

To combine the two pieces of this pendant and finish it, follow these steps:

1. Place the copper piece on the steel block and put on your safety goggles. Use the hammer and center punch to make small dents in the four corners of

the copper. Don't make the holes too close to the edge.

2. Place the copper on your bench pin or scrap of wood. Drill holes in each of the four marked locations using the number 52 drill bit. Lubricate the drill bit before drilling each hole.

3. Clean the burs from the back of the copper using the needle files or a drill bit larger than the holes.

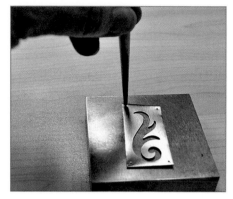

Make dents with the center punch in the copper pendant.

4. Take one of the ¼-inch (6.25 millimeter) pieces of 14-gauge round wire, and file it smooth on one end. Check it in one of the rivet holes for fit. Use pliers to hold the rivet wire. To enlarge the hole, use the scribe in a twirling motion or use a round needle file. Continue until all rivets just fit through the holes—the fit should be very snug. Remove burs and sand the back of the copper to smooth it.

5. Place the copper piece on top of the silver piece, and adjust until the arrangement pleases you. Holding this position, place the marker in one of the holes to mark the silver below. Do this with the rest of the holes to mark the rivet locations on the silver. Set the copper piece aside.

6. Drill a hole in one of the marked rivet locations—not all of them. Smooth the bur on the back of the metal. Test one of the silver wires in the hole you just made. Refine the hole until the rivet fits snugly. Remove the rivet and set it aside.

7. Place the copper piece on top of the silver piece. Work one of the rivets through both holes. The entire rivet should be the thickness of the metal sandwich plus half. Cut off the excess wire from the back side of the pendant using metal shears. This helps keep errant marks from marring the front of your piece.

8. Place the metal sandwich on your bench block, making sure that there is an equal amount of wire protruding from both sides of your metal sandwich.

This layered pendant is wet from being dipped in patina solution.

Holding the metal sandwich in a floating position slightly above the bench block, tap the rivet a few times with your goldsmith's (or other) hammer. Flip the piece over, and tap a few more times. Continue flipping back and forth until the rivet head mushrooms. Finish smoothing down the rivet head with a larger hammer.

9. Realign the holes in the metal sandwich. Choose the farthest hole from the current rivet, and drill a hole in that location. Set the second rivet. After this, you can pierce the other two holes and set the rivets.

10. Sand the metal using the 320-grit and then the 400-grit sandpapers.

11. Add the jump ring to the pendant bail.

12. Clean the metal using Dawn and a brass-bristle brush, traveling in one direction.

13. Apply a liver of sulfur patina to your pendant, dipping it in and out of the patina several times and rinsing it with water in between dips to build the patina slowly.

14. Allow the metal to dry completely. There will be moisture trapped between the layers.

15. Rub the pendant with steel wool, traveling in one direction.

16. Apply two coats of wax to seal the finish.

Manhattan Harley Cuff Links

Elegance and grit blend in this cuff link design. Practice a simple chasing technique to get the tire tread and spoke detail similar to a motorcycle tire. The copper hub gives you practice sweat-soldering two different metals. This design makes a striking pair of earrings, too. Choose 22-gauge metal for the circles, and drill a small hole in the top of the completed discs to accommodate ear wires.

Materials:

- Two ¾-inch (2-centimeter) discs of 18-gauge sterling silver, annealed

- Two ¼-inch (.75-centimeter) discs of 22-gauge copper, annealed

- Two sterling silver cuff link findings

Setups: Torch (any torch); filing, sanding, and finishing; utility; plus 18-gauge steel or iron binding wire, dapping block and punches, bench block, ball-peen hammer, masonry nail filed to a chiseled point, and a 3-inch (7.5-centimeter) long nail.

These silver cuff links have a copper accent.

(© Paul D'Andrea)

Solder the Copper Hubs to the Silver Discs

The first part of the process is to solder the two metal discs together. Follow these steps:

1. File the perimeter of the discs using the number 2 flat file to smooth the edges. Sand the front-facing surface of the discs using 220-grit, 320-grit, and then 400-grit sandpapers. After sanding, handle the discs by the edges.

2. Locate the center point of the larger discs, and make a dot there using a permanent marker. This is where you will solder the copper hub.

Sweat-solder copper to silver with the torch flame.

3. Apply flux to the back of the copper discs and the front of the silver discs.

4. Add three or four small chips of medium solder to the small copper discs. Heat the metal using the torch, until the solder slumps. Don't overheat the copper, or oxides will form, preventing the solder from flowing.

5. Heat the silver discs until the flux turns translucent. Add a little more flux to the copper.

6. Using fine-point tweezers, flip the small discs onto the center of the larger discs. Focusing the heat of the torch around the outside edge of the silver discs, heat one of the assemblies. Watch for the copper disc to settle. The solder will melt soon after, within seconds.

7. As soon as you see the solder flow, remove the heat. If the smaller disc slides out of position, gently move it back with your solder pick. Repeat the soldering process for the other disc.

8. Cool the metal slightly, quench it, and pickle it for five minutes.

9. Neutralize the metal and rinse it, and then clean all sides of the metal using a brass brush and soapy water.

Add Texture and Shape the Cuff Links

Now it's time to add some character to your cuff links by adding texture. Follow these steps:

1. Place a disc on the bench block. Using a ball-peen hammer and the masonry nail filed to a broad, chiseled point, create the spokes. Arrange the spokes in a cross-hatched pattern radiating from the center of the copper disc.

Texture the inner part of the silver discs.

2. Create the outer design by striking the head of the 3-inch (7.62-centimeter) nail placed on its side. Overlap the marks to create a tread pattern.

3. Anneal the metal, being careful not to reflow the solder. Quench it, and then pickle it for five minutes. Neutralize, rinse, and dry it.

4. Place the metal face down into a 1¼-inch (3.18-centimeter) concavity in the dapping block, with a piece of paper towel under it to protect the design. Dome the metal slightly. I started using a wooden punch, and then switched to a metal punch to complete the slight amount of doming needed.

5. Clean the back side of the discs to prepare them for soldering. Make a small mark in the center of each disc using a permanent marker. This will be the location of the cuff link finding.

6. Sand the backs of each of the findings using 400-grit sandpaper.

7. Create soldering props for your discs. You'll need these to keep your assembly together during soldering. Cut binding wire and form it into small coils. Make six of these and place them on your soldering surface.

8. Brush the back of the discs and the back of the cuff link findings with a thin layer of paste flux. Place the cuff link finding on the back of the disc. Prop chips of easy solder around the findings, creating little bridges to connect the back of the discs to the findings.

9. Light the torch and heat the soldering surface around the discs, allowing the flux to bubble. Reposition any errant chips of solder using your pick. When the flux clears, move the heat of the flame to the edge of the silver discs. Don't heat the finding directly, as this could melt it or

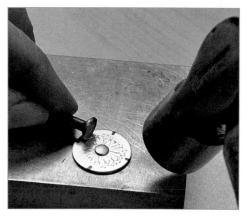

Use the side of a nail head to add texture.

Prop up the cuff links with wire before soldering the findings.

Rub steel wool over the completed cuff links.

damage the tension of the mechanism. Keep the flame moving, and watch for the solder to flow all around the finding. Repeat for the other disc assembly.

10. Allow the metal to air-cool. Then pickle the metal for five minutes, neutralize it, rinse it, and clean it with a brass brush and soapy water.

11. Apply a liver of sulfur patina to your cuff links.

12. Allow the patina to dry, and then rub the cuff links with steel wool to remove some of the patina.

13. Apply two layers of wax, buffing between each layer with a soft cloth.

Honeycomb Geometric Brooch

A simple rectangle takes on new dimensions when you add pierced geometric shapes. Hone your piercing, sawing, and soldering skills with this sleek brooch project. Customize your brooch by adding more or fewer geometric elements, as you choose. Go further, and create your own pattern of random geometric shapes. Just be sure to leave room to solder on your pin back! NuGold, a brass alloy, is featured as the rich-looking but low-cost gold-colored metal in the project. The brooch project also uses a premade pin finding.

This finished brass brooch is 2 inches (5 centimeters) long by ⅞ inches (2.25 centimeters) across.

(© Paul D'Andrea)

Materials:

- About 3 inches × 1 inch (7.5 centimeters × 2.5 centimeters) of 18- or 20-gauge NuGold sheet

- Three-piece pin catch set with pin stem at least 2 inches (5 centimeters) long

Setups: Torch (any torch), cutting and piercing, utility, plus ball-peen hammer, bench block, and number 56 drill bit or close to it.

Saw the Shapes

To cut out the pattern on the metal, follow these steps:

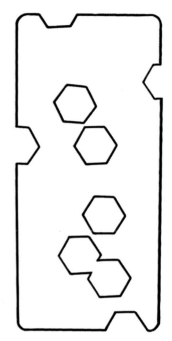

Copy this geometric pattern to create the Honeycomb brooch.

1. Sand the piece of NuGold with 220-grit wet/dry sandpaper to clean it and help the glue to adhere. You can also pick the best part of the metal for your design once you've sanded it. For this project, travel the sandpaper in one direction, vertically, back and forth over the surface. This will be the direction of the final, satin finish.

2. Copy the pattern and trim away the excess paper, leaving a ¼-inch (.75-centimeter) border around the edge of the pattern. Make two copies of the template provided. Reserve the extra copy for practice or in case of a mishap.

3. Glue the pattern onto the clean metal. Align at least one edge of the pattern to one edge of the metal and you won't have to cut that part out. Smooth out any air bubbles that may become trapped. Allow it to dry for several minutes.

4. Place your metal on the steel block and put on your safety goggles. Use the hammer on the center punch to make small dents in all of the interior honeycomb shapes. You won't need to do this on the outer shapes.

5. Drill holes, using the small dents as drilling guides. Lubricate the drill bit by turning the drill and placing the bit lightly into the lubricant. For each hole drilled, apply more lubricant.

6. Load the jeweler's saw with a 3/0 (or finer) saw blade, and tighten one of the nuts on the saw frame. Thread the other end of the blade into one of the drilled holes in your metal. Place the end of the blade into the other nut on the saw frame and tighten it. The front of the brooch must be facing up.

7. Slowly, with long strokes, saw out the first of the geometric shapes. Take your time and develop a rhythm. When you get to each corner, move the saw frame up and down like the needle on a sewing machine, and slowly turn the metal without engaging the teeth. When you've stopped turning the metal, you can engage the teeth again, moving forward.

Use the jeweler's saw to cut the geometric shapes.

File the interior geometric shapes.

> **ARTISAN TIP**
>
> Don't go overboard with filing. Even small, fine needle files can remove a lot of metal and change crisp, geometric edges into rounded curves.

8. After each shape is sawed out, loosen one of the nuts on the saw frame, and move to the next area. Complete all of the sawing for the interior shapes.

9. Cut the main portion of the exterior shape using your metal shears, and then use your jeweler's saw to cut out the exterior honeycomb shapes. Take a moment to shake out your shoulders, wrists, and hands from time to time. Cut out all of the exterior shapes.

10. Remove the pattern from your metal using soapy water. Rinse and dry the metal.

11. Use the needle files to gently refine the inside of the cutouts.

12. Pre-finish the metal using sandpaper. Flip the metal face down onto your work surface with a paper napkin underneath to keep the face from becoming scratched. Sand through the progression of wet/dry sandpapers: 220, then 320, then 400. Travel in one direction, up and down the brooch. Turn the metal over and repeat on the front side. This sanding will help make the final satin finish easy to achieve.

Solder the Pin Catch Assembly

To attach the pin catch and finish the brooch, follow these steps:

1. Use soapy water and a brass brush to clean your metal well, traveling in one direction with the brush. Dry your metal with a clean hand towel or paper towels. Set it on your work surface, face down.

2. On the back of the brooch, measure ¼ inch (.75-centimeter) down from the top and measure to the center. Make a mark using your permanent marker. Don't touch the metal with your fingers, only the marker. This is where the hinge portion of

your pin will be soldered. Make a similar mark for the catch. Place it ¼ inch (.64 centimeter) from the bottom of the brooch and in the center. These measurements don't have to be perfect, but they must line up well enough that your pin will function when assembled.

3. Open and close the catch part of the pin catch to make sure it works well. Leave the pin catch in the open position. Take a tiny piece of dirt or grit and stick it in the open mouth of the pin catch to prevent solder from flowing up into the catch.

4. Lightly sand the bottom of the pin catch and the pin hinge.

5. Apply flux in a thin, even layer only to the bottom of these pieces. Holding the pieces in your tweezers may help you. Set both of the pieces on their sides on your soldering surface.

6. Apply a thin, even layer of paste flux right over the marks you made on the back of the brooch. Set the brooch on your soldering surface.

7. Use tweezers to place the pin hinge on the top mark on your brooch. Then use the tweezers to place two small pallions of easy silver solder on either side of the pin hinge. The solder chip must make a little bridge. One side touches the hinge and the other touches the brooch back. Do the same thing with the pin catch. Put it into position at the bottom of the brooch. The jaw will run parallel to the bottom of the brooch. The jaw can open either to the left or to the right, whatever is your preference.

8. Light the torch. Swirl the flame a few times around brooch. Then move the flame back and forth over the middle of the brooch. Keep your pick at the ready to move the solder back into

The red marks indicate where the hinge and catch of the pin back will be soldered.

The catch has been soldered on the brooch, and the hinge has been brushed with flux in preparation.

place as needed. Keep in mind that you can only do this when the heat is nearby, otherwise solder chips will stick to your pick. If that happens, move the flame closer until you're able to position the solder chip where it belongs.

9. When the flux turns clear, you can move the torch flame closer. Go to the pin hinge at the top of the brooch. Move the flame around the pin hinge, not directly on it. When you see the silver flash of melting solder, immediately move the flame away from that area. Repeat the soldering for the pin catch at the bottom of the brooch.

10. Air-cool the brooch for five minutes before quenching it. Then pickle the metal for five minutes, using copper tongs whenever placing or retrieving items from the pickle pot. Neutralize the metal, and rinse it in plain water.

11. Gently twist the pin catch and hinge to make sure they have been soldered securely. If you need to resolder, clean the metal with a brass brush or green scrubbing pad and repeat the previous steps for soldering. Make sure the catch still works, and remember to put some grit into the jaws of the catch to keep solder from flowing into it.

12. Assemble the pin. Place the brooch face down on a piece of cloth or paper toweling on your work surface. Place the pin stem into the pin hinge. Using chain-nose pliers, place the jaws of the pliers over the hinge, and lightly squeeze the hinge from both sides equally and at the same time.

13. If your pin stem is too long, trim it with cutting pliers. The end of the pin should come just inside the edge of your brooch back. File and sand the edges to a smooth point.

> **METAL MISHAP**
>
> If your metal becomes copper plated, you can make a super pickle solution to remove it. Get a small plastic or glass container and dip out some warm pickle from the pickle pot into it. Add hydrogen peroxide to make a 50/50 mixture. Place the brooch in the mixture. Leave it for two minutes. Don't leave items too long—they will quickly become pitted. Neutralize and rinse your metal as usual. The super pickle reverts to normal-strength pickle once the bubbles dissipate. You can then add it back to the pickle pot.

14. Use a brass brush and soapy water to clean the brooch on both sides, traveling in one direction. Gently work the brass brush around the pin assembly. Dry the brooch well, again traveling in one direction with your cloth.

15. Use a clean, soft, dry cloth to wax the brooch. Apply two coats of Renaissance wax or Johnson Paste Wax, buffing gently yet vigorously in one direction to get a soft sheen.

Captured Canyon Gemstone Prong Setting

This Oregon thunдеregg agate cabochon caught my attention during a visit to my local lapidary, Jox Rox. The simple prong setting is elevated by adding the fancy spiral element to the pendant and coiled jump ring bail. Pair this pendant with the Ginger sterling neck wire for a stunning duo. For a simpler approach, eliminate the spiral and coiled jump ring and replace them with smaller loops.

Materials:

- Large triangular-shaped stone, approximately 40 millimeters along each side

- 16 inches (40.75 centimeters) of 16-gauge round sterling silver wire, annealed

- 6 inches (15.25 centimeters) of 18-gauge round sterling silver wire, annealed

This gemstone pendant is set in silver prongs.

(© Paul D'Andrea)

Setups: Torch (any torch), pliers, utility, patina, plus t-pins, metal shears, ³⁄₈-inch (1-centimeter) and ¹⁄₂-inch (1.25-centimeter) dowel rods, masonry nail sharpened to a chisel point, and paper and pencil.

> **ARTISAN TIP**
>
> You don't have to use a triangular 40-millimeter gemstone for this project. Adapt the recipe to suit your ingredients! You can modify a prong setting to suit many sizes and shapes of cabochon gemstones. Lay out your design on paper and trace around your stone as this project illustrates. Make sure you provide four to six prongs to hold your gemstone in place, and add any other embellishments to your design. Enjoy the results with pride!

Design the Setting and Assemble the Pieces

To make this gemstone prong setting, follow these steps:

1. Place your gemstone on a piece of paper, and trace around it using a pencil. Remove the stone. Six prongs were used on the sample project. That meant I used three pieces of U-shaped wire to create six prongs. The bottom parts of the U shapes touch one another, creating points of contact for soldering. Draw the location of the U-shaped prongs for your stone on your paper.

2. Cut the 16-gauge round wire into three 2½-inch (6.25-centimeter) pieces, leaving an 8-inch (20.25-centimeter) piece of wire for the coil at the top.

3. Bend one of the 2½-inch (63.50 millimeter) lengths of wire over a half-inch dowel rod, creating a U shape. Repeat for the other two pieces of 2½-inch (63.50 millimeters) wire.

4. Wrap the 8-inch (203.2 millimeter) piece of wire around the dowel rod. Slide the completed coil off of the dowel rod. Using your fingers and pliers, flip up one end of the coil to create a figure-eight effect, with a single loop at one end and the rest of the coiled wire at the other.

5. Lay the pieces of shaped wire on your paper. Adjust the wires with your fingers, so they make contact with one another. There should be two points of

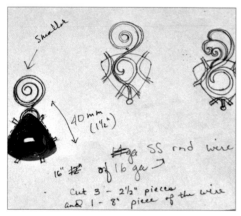

Sketch out a design for a setting that fits your gemstone.

contact for each of the prongs and for the lower portion of the spiral element. The upper portion of the spiral touches at one point, too. Leave enough room in the spiral to accommodate the fancy jump ring bail, which will be added later.

6. Place the gemstone on the assembly for a test fit, and make any adjustments needed so that the prongs capture the stone in two places on each side. Set the stone aside.

Solder the Prongs and Set the Stone

Follow these steps to finish your setting:

1. Take the assembly to the soldering station, and lay it out on a soldering block, preserving the arrangement. Place t-pins to hold the assembly in place.

2. Apply paste flux and hard solder chips to all points of contact. I used a toothpick to apply the flux. A good assembly makes soldering easy, so take your time with this.

3. Light your torch and heat the soldering block around the assembly. After the flux has stopped bubbling, move the torch closer to the metal, keeping the flame moving at all times.

4. When the flux turns clear, focus the heat near one of the joins. Heat until the solder flows, and then move to the next area. Keep your soldering pick at the ready to make adjustments to solder or wires as needed.

5. Quench, pickle, neutralize, and rinse the assembly. Check that all points of contact are joined. Reflux and resolder as needed.

6. Clean the assembly with a brass brush and soapy water.

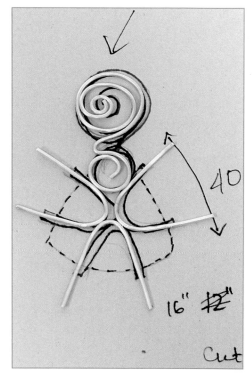

Match up the cut and shaped wires to your design.

Solder the silver wire together.

Mark the area around the gemstone to indicate where to bend the prongs.

Use a nail to make dents in the silver pendant.

Cut excess wire using metal shears.

7. Place the assembly on your work surface, and place the gemstone on it. Use your fingers to make any needed adjustments to the prongs. With the gemstone in position, use a fine-point permanent marker to mark the metal where the stone touches. This is where you'll bend the prongs. Set the stone aside.

8. Place the assembly on your bench block. Make creases in the wire at the marked locations by placing the masonry nail on the marks, and then hitting it with a ball-peen hammer. Don't hit so hard that the metal is cut in half.

9. Make sure the prongs are long enough to come about one-third the way up the side of the stone. Cut off the excess, and file the prongs down a bit using flat files and needle files. The prongs should be slightly thinned on the inside where they touch the gemstone and smooth on the outside.

10. Shape and refine the spiral using your fingers. Place it on the bench block and gently work-harden it using a planishing hammer.

11. Make the fancy jump ring bail by coiling 6 inches (152.40 centimeters) of 18-gauge round wire around a ⅜-inch (.97-centimeter) dowel rod.

12. Using round-nose pliers, make a very small loop at each end of the coil. Refine the shape of the coil with flat-nose pliers, slightly opening them to get a flared shape. Work the jump ring bail around the top part of the pendant spiral.

13. Bend the prong tips slightly with flat-nosed pliers to create a slight hook at the very tip of the prong. This will help allow the length of the prong, once bent, to contact the curved top of the gemstone.

14. Work the stone into the prong setting, and complete the work of turning the prongs toward the stone. Use flat-nose and chain-nose pliers until the

prongs close over the stone, holding it in place. Use the blunt end of a cut-off toothbrush to smooth the prongs further.

15. Apply a liver of sulfur patina to the pendant. It won't hurt a stone as hard as the agate. But don't use LOS patina on turquoise or softer stones as it may stain the stones.

Coil the wire to create the bail.

Use a cut-off toothbrush to set a gemstone.

Glossary

abrasives   Natural or man-made grit adhered to a backing material, used to make sandpapers or other items for use in smoothing metal.

alloy   Two or more metals melted together.

anneal   To soften metal and increase malleability through the use of applied heat.

avoirdupois ounce   Unit of measurement that Americans use for precious metals.

bail   The mechanism that attaches a pendant to a necklace.

base metal   A nonferrous, nonprecious metal, such as brass, copper, or nickel.

bench pin   A strip of wood that projects from a bench or work surface and is used to facilitate metalworking activities.

bezel   A gemstone setting that consists of a thin band of metal soldered to a back plate.

bezel cup   The metal container that holds the gem in a bezel setting. It is made from wire soldered to a back plate.

bezel pusher   Polished steel tools in various shapes that are used to push or rub a bezel wire over a gemstone in a bezel setting.

bezel wire   A thin strip of metal used in a gemstone setting.

broach   A small, slender, five-sided, very sharp cutting tool that is used to enlarge holes.

buff tops   Cabochons with flat tops.

burnishing   Smoothing the surface of metal by rubbing it with tools made of metal, hard plastic, horn, or other materials.

carat   A unit of measurement, typically for gemstones, that is equal to one-fifth of a gram.

cabochon   A gemstone that hasn't been cut into facets. Typically offered as a smooth-top, smooth-sided stone, but that can vary greatly.

chasing   Working a design onto the front of metal using gentle, measured force to displace the material, creating the desired imagery.

chuck key   A small device used to tighten or loosen the chuck opening of a drill.

cold connection   Connecting two or more items mechanically, without the use of heat. Examples are rivets and tabs and slots.

conductivity   Ability to transport electrical energy and heat. Metals are highly conductive.

course   One full round of hammering with overlapping blows in a circular pattern.

crazy hairs   Frilly rubber wheels impregnated with ceramic aluminum oxide polishing compound. Their proper name is 3M radial bristle discs.

curing   The solidification process of a liquid turning solid.

dapping   Forming metal into domed circular shapes through the use of a dapping block.

dapping block   A block of wood or steel containing circular concavities used to form metal.

dapping punch   Also known as dapping tools, these are often sold as a set with dapping blocks to match the depressions on the block.

dead soft   Most malleable form of metal. It can be easily bent with your hands.

depletion gilding   The repeated torch heating and cooling of sterling silver to burn off some copper and build up a layer of fine silver. Also called "bringing up the silver" or "raising the fine silver."

depressing   Forcing metal into a shaped contour, usually with the help of another tool.

ductile   The ability of metal to be stretched to a certain degree before breaking.

enamel   Powdered colored glass used in enameling and fused to a metal surface.

end caps   Terminations used at either end of a necklace that serve as a means to attach a clasp or closure.

escapement file   Also known as a square-handled needle file. This file is smaller than a hand file but larger than a needle file.

etchant   A chemical used to produce a design on the surface of metal.

etching   A chemical process of applying a design by using acid to remove selectively exposed areas of the metal surface.

fabricated bail   Mechanism that is soldered or riveted to the pendant to attach it to a necklace.

faceted   Gemstones that have been cut into geometric planes to reflect light. These cuts can be made by hand or by machine, and the stones can be either natural or man-made.

ferrous   A metal that contains iron.

findings   Jewelry components that perform useful functions, such as ear wires, clasps, catches, pins, and hinges.

firescale   Also called fire stain. A purplish or dark-colored stain on sterling silver or other metals that is created when metal is heated, trapping oxides within.

flexible shaft machine   A motorized machine consisting of a small hanging motor unit connected to a handpiece by a rotating wire covered in a flexible rubber sheath. The motor is operated by a variable-speed dial or foot pedal and the handpiece accepts various burs and bits. Also known as flex shaft.

flux   A liquid or paste used to prevent oxides from forming during soldering.

foldforming   Technique invented by Charles Lewton-Brain that enables metalsmiths to create dimensional forms using thin sheets of metal, forging hammers, and torch heat.

forging   The process of hammering metal to thin, thicken, or alter its shape.

forming   The process of bending metal to change its shape.

full-hard   Stiffer than half-hard, this type of metal holds its shape well, but you can still bend it using tools.

fuming   Exposing metal to vapors, such as ammonia fumes, in order to produce a color tint, typically a blue-green color.

fusing   Joining metals through direct application of high heat.

gauge   A measuring standard for the thickness of sheet metal and the diameter of wire.

hallmark   Official symbols used for marking precious metal jewelry.

half-hard   Malleable enough to be bent with tools or even with your hands and some force.

hand file   The longest and widest type of file. Hand files come in many different shapes, including flat, half-round, and barette.

heat sink   A substance that absorbs heat.

integral bail   Part of a pendant design that connects the pendant to a necklace.

jump ring   A wire circle used in jewelry making as a means of connection.

liver of sulfur   A blend of potassium sulfides used as a darkening patina for metal.

malleable   The ability of metal to be bent and shaped.

mandrel   Forms around which metal may be shaped.

mordant   Any chemical used in the metal etching process.

needle file   A small, thin file meant for delicate tasks.

nonferrous   A metal that does not contain iron. Traditionally, metals used in jewelry making are nonferrous.

oxides   Heat combined with oxygen forms oxides, which inhibit the flow of solder.

pallions   Small chips or pieces of solder.

patina   Surface color on metal achieved either over a long period of time or through the use of applied chemicals or heat.

peg   A wire that fits snugly into a half-drilled pearl or other object and is soldered to a back plate or cup.

pickle   A solution of acid and water used to remove flux and oxides from metal after annealing or soldering operations.

planishing   Pounding the surface of metal with a polished hammer to smooth it.

pumice   Porous, volcanic rock. Large pebbles are used in a pan while soldering to protect the surrounding areas from heat. You also can use powdered pumice to degrease and polish metal.

polishing compounds   A fine abrasive and a binder, such as wax or grease, used in polishing metal. Also known as buffing compounds.

polishing stick   Pieces of wood with leather or cloth attached, used to facilitate polishing operations. May be used with a polishing compound.

precious metal   A rare and costly metal, such as silver or gold.

prong   Wire that is pushed over a gemstone to secure it in place. A group of prongs are arranged in a pattern to create a setting.

repoussé   Working a design onto metal from the back by pushing metal outward from behind.

resist   A coating applied to metal that withstands the effects of chemicals.

riffler file   A file with one or two curved ends.

ring clamp   Tool for holding small items that has two working ends with a hinge in the middle and a tapered wedge.

rivet   A type of cold connection that uses a short length of wire or tubing to connect two other items. It also is used decoratively.

rolling mill   A machine using two adjustable, opposing steel rollers to reduce the gauge of metal sheet and wire or to imprint a texture onto a metal sheet.

rose cut   A cross between a faceted stone and a cabochon that features triangular facets on the top and a smooth bottom.

sanding stick   Pieces of wood with sandpaper attached, used to facilitate sanding operations.

sandpaper   An abrasive medium adhered to a backing material that is used for sanding or smoothing surfaces.

slots and tabs   A type of cold connection in which a pierced opening, or *slot*, matches a protrusion, or *tab*. The tab is inserted in the slot and bent over to connect two areas or secure found objects.

scoring   The removal of metal along a line to create a sharp bend or crease.

solder   A metal alloy used to join pieces of metal through the use of heat. Solder contains a certain percentage of the same metal it is used to connect. General categories of solder for metalsmiths are extra easy, easy, medium, hard, extra hard, and eutectic.

soldering   Connecting two pieces of metal by melting a metal alloy that is of a lower melting point than the metals it joins. This alloy is known as solder.

spot price   The cash price of a commodity, such as a troy ounce of precious metals, on any given day. The spot price doesn't include transportation, storage costs, other expenses, or value-added services such as turning an ingot into sheet metal or wire.

stop bath   Neutralizing mixture to halt action of acid or base chemicals.

sweeps catch   A piece of fabric or leather attached to the work surface used for capturing bits of metal or other small items.

sweeps drawer   A pull-out tray in a jeweler's bench used for capturing metal shavings and dust. Also known as a sweeps tray.

temper   The relative hardness or softness of metal.

thrumming   A method of polishing metal using one or multiple length of string impregnated with a polishing compound.

troy weight   A system of measurement for precious metals like gold and silver.

tube setting   A measured length of hollow silver is soldered to the body of a jewelry item. A seat is cut in it to accommodate a gem.

upsetting   Hammering each end of a rivet to widen it and keep the rivet in place.

work hardening   Stiffening of metal and changing the temper through the application of force, such as bending, twisting, pulling, or compressing. Examples would be hammering or stamping metal.

More About Metal

Troy Weight

Troy ounce is the standard of measurement for precious metals, such as silver, gold, and platinum.

24 grains = 1 pennyweight (dwt.)	12 ounces = 1 troy pound
20 dwt. = 1 troy ounce	5,760 grains = 1 troy pound

Avoirdupois Weight

Avoirdupois is the standard of measurement to use for base metals, such as copper, brass, aluminum, and nickel silver.

16 grams = 1 ounce avoirdupois	16 ounces = 7,000 grams
16 ounces = 1 pound avoirdupois	

Weight Conversion

Multiply 1.09714 to convert troy ounces to avoirdupois.

Multiply by .91146 to convert avoirdupois to troy ounces.

Metric Conversion

Millimeters to feet × .00328

Inches to centimeters × 2.54

Millimeters to inches × .03937

Inches to millimeters × 25.4

Circumference Formula

To determine the circumference of a circle, multiply the diameter by 3.1416.

Copper and Copper Alloys

The Copper Development Association hosts an informative and useful website containing in-depth detail on copper and copper alloys such as brass, bronze, and nickel silver.

To learn more about the chemical composition and designation system for copper and copper alloys, go to copper.org. The following numbering system is used to identify copper alloys:

Coppers (C10100 to C15999)

High copper alloys (C16000 to C19999)

Brasses (C20000 to C49999)

Bronzes (C50000 to C69999)

Copper nickels (C70000 to C73499)

Nickel silvers (C73500 to C79999)

The metals that are used in the different alloys are listed on the Copper Development Association site as well.

Mohs Scale of Hardness

Mineral	Hardness	Scratch Test
Talc	1	Can be easily scratched with fingernail
Plaster (gypsum)	2	Can be scratched with fingernail
Limestone, pearl	3	Can be scratched with coin
Fluorite, rhodochrosite	4	Can be scratched easily with knife
Apatite	5	Can be scratched with knife
Feldspar, moonstone, peridot	6	Can be scratched with steel file, can scratch glass
Quartz, citrine, amethyst, garnet, emerald	7	Easily scratches metal and glass
Topaz	8	Scratches quartz, softer stones
Ruby, sapphire	9	Scratches topaz
Diamond	10	Scratches ruby

Metal Thickness Recommendations

Gauge	Used For
14, 16	Band rings, men
16, 18	Band rings, women
10, 12, 14	Round wire rings, men or women
28, 30, 32	Bezel wire for setting cabochons
19	Earring posts
19, 20, 21	Ear wires
16, 18	Round or half-round wire for making prongs
22, 24	Foldforming for any jewelry items
14, 16, 18, 20	Sheet metal for cuff style bracelet
10, 12, 14, 16	Wire for cuff or bangle style bracelet
16, 18, 20, 22	Round wire for making jump rings
14, 16	Round or square wire for making clasps
14, 16	Brass or sterling wire for pin stems
16, 18	Nickel silver* for pin stems
18, 20, 22, 24	Stainless steel wire for pin stems

*Nickel silver does not contain any silver.

Gauge and Drill Bit Sizes

B&S*	Gauge*	Millimeters	Inches	Drill Size
2	6.54	.258	$\frac{1}{4}$	
4	5.19	.204	6	6
6	4.11	.162	$\frac{5}{32}$	20
8	3.25	.128	$\frac{1}{8}$	30
10	2.59	.102	38	
12	2.06	.081	$\frac{5}{64}$	46
14	1.63	.064	$\frac{1}{16}$	51
16	1.30	.051	54	
18	1.02	.040	56	
19	.914	.036	60	
20	.812	.032	$\frac{1}{32}$	65
21	.711	.028	67	
22	.635	.025	70	
24	.508	.020	74	
26	.406	.016	$\frac{1}{64}$	77
28	.034	.012	79	

Brown & Sharpe

Saw Blade Recommendations

These recommendations are not based upon industry standards, but upon personal preference for finer blades.

Gauge	Blade Size
12, 14	1, 1/0, 2/0
16, 18	1/0, 2/0, 3/0
20, 22	2/0, 3/0, 4/0
24, 26	3/0, 4/0, 5/0

Index